Past Forward

The Art & Science of Saving Houses

Mark Russell

Told by D. L. Coughlan

For Alex

Like many things in life, I unwittingly saved the best for later.
When I was 40, the birth of our son inspired me to start living again.
Seeing things through his young eyes teaches Lynn and me to live each
day knowing that the best is yet to come.

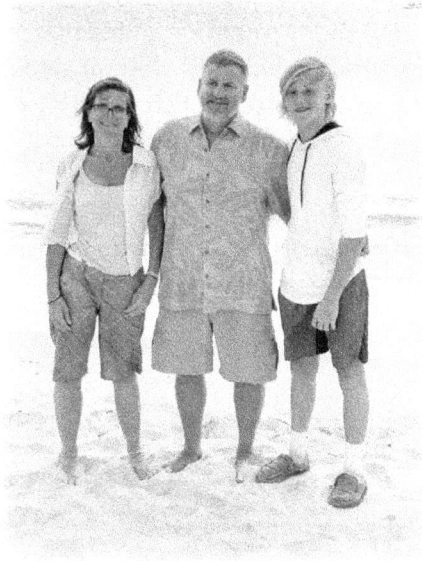

FOREWORD

This book is written for a wide spectrum of readers, from people with a casual interest in the subject matter to those who want to dig deeper. Two elements have been included to make it easy for you to define your own journey through the book.

First, you'll find plenty of stories. Part One is a collection of stories, while the remainder of the book weaves in anecdotes to illuminate topics. In these later chapters, stories are set apart on the page in italics to help you find them. If you like stories, you may gravitate to these tales before (or even instead of) reading other sections. To further pique your interest, chapter and section headings throughout the book include images of homes I've lived in or renovated, a few childhood sketches, and even some of my tattoos.

Second, the chapters about running a business and understanding home construction include a lot of important details but they may not be for everyone. If you want to sail through these sections and get to the juicy stuff in Part Five more quickly, just focus on the headers, statements, and Mark-It tips, all noted in bold.

Everyone likes to have choices in life and reading a book is no different. Forge your own path. Enjoy.

PROLOGUE

BUYER BEWARE. SELLER IS A FLIPPER.

Those six words appeared in capital letters at the top of a recent home inspection report. A buddy of mine was representing the seller of the house, which had been renovated. The buyers had fallen in love with the house and were ready to pull the trigger. They hired an inspector to help them identify issues and provide peace of mind. Yet, before conducting a review of the house, the inspector wrote six words on the report that might as well have said: BEWARE OF VICIOUS DOG! GO AWAY! Fear was injected into the situation, and the buyers backed out.

Maybe that is exactly what needed to happen. We'll never know.

I do know that a lot of confusion exists in our industry. Everyone interprets things differently. What does it mean to rehab, renovate, or update a house? What does it mean to flip it? Those questions are answered in different ways by buyers, sellers, inspectors, real estate professionals, rehabbers, flippers, and you.

These days, television has shaped our perception of flippers. Smiling TV personalities create quality work with amazing results for gushing customers, thanks to behind-the-scenes efforts and artful editing. Unfortunately, they also paint an unrealistic view of what can be accomplished by suggesting that anyone can do it. In real life, flippers often do the absolute minimum to fix or mask problems and get houses back on the market as quickly as possible. They might paint over smoke damage, cover a leak with sheetrock, or hide inferior products. Not every flipper does this, but it happens. Some just don't know better.

That's not me. I'm in the business of saving houses from ultimate demise after they've been neglected, abandoned, or left to rot in the elements. When I discover one of these forlorn gems, my first thoughts are: How can I turn it into a home again? How can I make it as new as possible? How can I give it a second chance at life? Along with giving another family a home, a house recovery might remove blight in the neighborhood, increase surrounding home values, or elevate the desirability of a street.

This book gives voice to the behind-the-scenes realities of our industry, but it's not a learn-everything-possible-about-rehabbing manual. It is a collection of experiences, an acknowledgement of challenges, and a labor of love. It reveals the value of getting a heck of a deal on a house that became a home when the decision was made to save it. That's how I view my work. It's a rescue effort.

BUYER DON'T WORRY. THIS SELLER CARES.

PART ONE

THE FOUNDATION

Whether it's a house or life itself,
a solid foundation can make all the difference.

3

CHAPTER 1

Why Did I Write This Book?

This book ventures beyond *how-to*, focusing more on *what-to*—as in *what to* expect, *what to* avoid, *what to* know, and *what to* appreciate. A solid foundation plus a good structure usually equals a worthy house, even if everything else needs to be redone. It won't be a new home built from scratch, but that's fine because older homes tend to have good bones.

Let me start by telling you what this book is *not*.

It's not … a how-to manual for flipping houses. God knows there is enough information in TV shows and everyday conversations to lure people into a business they know nothing about only to lead them on a path of financial ruin. I would prefer to talk you out of that.

It's not … a buyer's guide for purchasing a rehabbed home. You might find some of that here, but there's more to it.

It's not … an attempt to encourage—or discourage—those who want to get into the rehabbing business. While this book could inspire either of those decisions, that's not my main purpose.

I'm writing this book because stories are made to be told. They are part of my DNA, and quite frankly, they've been piling up for years. Many of my stories are actual experiences with buyers, sellers, and other people who have crossed my path. Some are funny, some are heartbreaking, some are costly. Collectively, they are teaching moments that landed me where I am today.

An authentic story paints a picture that cannot be captured through a camera lens. Before-and-after photographs don't convey the exploits of finding the house, developing a plan, creating the budget, agonizing over what the budget won't allow, working with contractors, dealing with unforeseen problems, being at the mercy of weather, laboring over permits, worrying through inspections, overcoming obstacles, and, ultimately, delivering a home. Pictures show the aftermath; stories reveal the blood, sweat, and tears.

I'm in the business of change, and that requires me to balance an appreciation for past craftsmanship with the promise of ongoing innovation. Construction techniques ebb and flow over time. In the 1800s, a home's weight was carried by a tree-trunk-sized piece of lumber suspended on rugged posts. By the mid-1900s, that method was replaced with a steel I-beam that later became the laminated (LVL) beam used today. Each material worked fine, so why change? It comes down to one thing, my friend. Price.

The bottom line is that a new house isn't more or less desirable than an updated one. It's just different, and you need to know the facts. In many cases, an older home may be more solid than anything you could find on the market today. Appearing shiny and new in its updated glory, a rescued house may stand on an old foundation with a structure comprised of yesterday's materials, codes, and construction principles. That doesn't make it inferior or less valuable. In fact, it may have been founded in tried-and-true practices that cut fewer corners and showcased more details.

Consider the story of a 170-year-old house. It's not new. It was built with 170-year-old lumber and 170-year-old nails on a 170-year-old foundation. When a new buyer decides to make that 170-year-old house a home, it will get a 21st century update but its bones remain the same.

We cannot change the aged steel, hand-hewn lumber, or pine plank floors in that 170-year-old home, and we wouldn't want to. By painstakingly salvaging every extraordinary, funky imperfection, we can nudge the house along, transforming classic features into modern-day benefits.

We can install a central HVAC system, improved plumbing, and new light fixtures. We can cover plaster with drywall, making it smooth and paintable. We can remove walls to create a master suite, and open the kitchen to the family room. With granite countertops, upscale kitchen cabinets, and sparkling appliances, we can bring spaces to life under custom LED lighting. In the expanded master bathroom, we can enclose a multi-head shower behind sparkling glass doors. These new features are beautiful and cosmetic. They are the jewelry people interact with daily. But they are not the house.

The house is still 170 years old.

When a 170-year-old house like the one in our story is given a new lease on life, it will thrive with the right owner or fail in the wrong hands. If you own a house like this or are thinking about renovating one, consider yourself lucky and understand what it means. Do you have the passion to listen to the house and determine if it's truly the right fit? While the house can be customized to meet a new era of expectations, it may require special maintenance and extra care. Do you have the stamina for that?

It would be impossible to reproduce the history and passion of that 170-year-old house, but as rehabbers, we have the opportunity—and perhaps even the responsibility—to preserve its character. It isn't easy for a house to settle into its surroundings. Costing four times as much to build, a new home would take decades to become as comfortable on its foundation. It must weather storms, endure heat, tolerate updates, and withstand neglect. Trees and shrubs will keep it company through the years, but it takes time for them to bond. A 170-year-old-house has experienced all of this and more.

Rescued homes are true miracles. They are time capsules ready to start over with a new generation of humans. I'm in the business of acknowledging their differences, correcting their problems, and accentuating their goodness. That's why I'm writing this book. These homes are unique gems. And, since they can't speak for themselves, someone has to do it. It might as well be me.

CHAPTER 2

Childhood and Quirky Stories

In many ways, my future was driven by unexpected encounters with ordinary things like eye tests, wood scraps, and bulletin boards. Through it all, I learned that the right teachers can be life-changing and Brady was my hero. Mike, that is, not Tom.

I grew up in Clinton, Maryland in the late 1960s and early 1970s, when homes didn't have computers and kids actually played outside. My brother, two sisters, and I were typical siblings raised in a typical split-level house in a typical suburban Washington, D.C. neighborhood. Both of my parents worked full time. Mom handled data entry for the Census Bureau before moving on to a personnel position at Andrews Air Force Base. My dad was a sheet metal worker who crafted cupulas and cornices for expensive Georgetown homes in addition to working part time as a drafting instructor for the union.

Watching my father use the tools of his trade provided my first taste of a lifelong appetite for architecture. I loved to go to work with him in D.C. where he fashioned classic features for elite residences that still stand tall. The craftsmanship that went into those architectural creations was incredible, and I later realized it ignited a passion in me.

Eye Tests

As a keenly visual person, it is extraordinary that my early view of the world was dramatically out of focus. In elementary school at a time when the chalkboard was used for everything—and we were learning cursive—it was impossible for me to grasp anything written there. I'm legally blind without glasses. Trouble is, it took a long time for anyone to realize this.

School was difficult but I meandered along thinking everyone saw things as I did. I traced letters on the desk in front of me, but couldn't read or copy anything from the board. My handwriting was horrific and my recognition was so bad that I was soon labeled a slow learner. When my second-grade teacher recommended holding me back, my parents agreed. Humiliated, I watched my friends move on as I stayed back with younger kids who used to look up to me.

Then it happened. School vision exams became mandatory and it was my turn to be tested. Looking into the view finder, I saw a bright puff of light, dark shadowing, and no detail beyond one giant letter at the top. The technician twisted, turned, and focused little dials until finally I began to see letters and shapes that I had viewed only on paper at close range. I had no idea what this meant.

Next came the red barn, green grass, and white fence with a yellow ball that was supposed to be inside or outside the fence. Through the view finder, I saw fuzzy green and blobbish red with white blurry edges. I didn't see the fence or the ball. Then, something miraculous happened. As the technician twisted the dials, suddenly I could see the fence … and the ball … and the trim on the door … and the hay bale … and the rope. And—lo and behold—the ball moved in and out of the yard and I could see it all!

Turns out, no one had been seeing things as I was.

Having passed this test, I began to feel somewhat normal until I arrived home to learn that I needed an immediate appointment with an eye doctor. In later years, my parents translated what I didn't understand at the time. The technicians and school officials were blown away by the fact that I had made it as far as I had in life given my lack of depth perception and inability to discern details of any sort.

I was subjected to more tests at the eye doctor, where they flipped lenses and asked me to choose: A or B? A or B? as my view became clearer and crisper. None of this mattered until a few weeks later when my glasses arrived. Their thick rims and ridiculous Coke bottle lenses sent me into despair. In my mind, I could see my school status plummeting; it would have been better to chop off my arm.

Then I put on my glasses for the first time. Everything was different.

My brain was on overload and, feeling sick, I actually threw up during the car ride home. Arriving in the driveway, I peered at our house from a new vantage point. I was mesmerized by the numbers at the door, the details in the fluted columns, the individual slats on the shutters, and the subtle inconsistencies of texture and color in the white brick of our house. Looking around, I saw individual blades of grass, trees, leaves, and an explosion of details that came at me from every direction.

How was it possible that I didn't know—and everyone missed—I had been seeing things so differently? Year after year, I had celebrated Christmas with my family around a tree that was a puff ball explosion of multicolored lights. When the lights were off, I couldn't see it from the sofa at all. Of course I knew what the ornaments looked like; I had made many of them. Yet, I couldn't recognize one from across the room. Watching TV had been the same. I knew our reception wasn't great, so I didn't question the blurry images I saw from the floor where I watched. I figured my parents were viewing the same fuzzy scenes from their seats on the sofa.

My God, why hadn't this come out earlier?

I no longer cared about being the target of teasing at school. My world had changed. The dorkiness my friends saw in my glasses became my motivation to work harder and become stronger. I pushed through the embarrassment of failing a grade, attending class with kids who were younger than I was, and doing it all behind thick lenses that were almost always broken. If this sounds emotional, it was. Everything I thought I knew was suddenly different.

While that experience may or may not have altered my life in the long run, it certainly changed my ability to learn and excel after my second shot at second grade. Taking a swing at a ball finally made sense to me because I could actually see it coming. Despite—or perhaps because of—all this, I am a keenly visual person. I'm aware of details and feel compelled to discern and remember the unique characteristics of things around me. This experience shaped my perspective and, ironically, it gave me an incredible ability to see what others sometimes miss.

Wood Scraps, Tree Houses & Go-Karts

Around the age of nine, I discovered the pile of wood scraps my father had accumulated behind the house. It wasn't fireplace wood, just pieces of pallets, lumber, and nonsense. I used that stack of stuff to build anything imaginable, from treehouses and forts to go-karts and lean-tos. No sooner had I built something than I would pull it apart and turn it into something else.

My father and grandfather taught me a few things about tools but most of my construction knowledge came from hands-on experience. After falling out of a few trees, surviving clubhouse roof collapses, and crashing into curbs, I learned the principles of construction. Survival depended on discovering how structures could be supported and how they couldn't, or how things go together and how they don't.

Perched at the top of a hill, our community of Crestview was aptly named. All roads in the neighborhood sloped downhill toward our house and the elementary school that was practically in our backyard. It was the perfect place to launch my latest scrap-pile-generated vehicle that began as a wheel nailed to a 2x4. Over time, I created a fleet of go-karts with varying abilities to negotiate the hill, leading to ultimate encounters with the curb, parked cars, and who knows what else. Each time a new creation crashed and fell apart, I tried a different way to fix it. By merging this with that, I continuously designed better ideas. There were no TV shows or YouTube videos to provide answers so I figured things out by using nails, hammers, wood, bike parts, and big wheel tires. Creating a new adventure was as easy as nailing different things together. With the building boom in full swing, I pilfered windows, doors, and more from old homes in our neighborhood that had been demolished in preparation for new construction.

This is how I spent my days and it wasn't long before I dragged others into my building adventures. The twins across the street—Deb and Dottie O'Clair—turned out to be talented apprentices who would help me create clubhouses, furniture, and a variety of ridiculous things. Having stumbled upon the value of a well-designed plan, I labored over detailed drawings that we transformed into elaborate structures. Using brick and plastic, we built a pond inside our clubhouse, filled it with water, and created a home for the duck we caught.

In addition to the wood scraps, we had a log cabin kit from Toys "R" Us with a center door and two side windows. It was made of real wood with a metal roof, not the pop-together plastic you find today. I'm sure the Toys "R" Us people didn't realize how versatile their product was; we took it apart numerous times, reassembling it into a condo in a tree, a fort in the backyard, and a lean-to on the side of the house. Later, we added a second story, transforming it into an office building. Depending on the day, that log cabin was anything we wanted it to be.

Sketching Out a Future

During this time, if one of us kids needed to be somewhere—like a football game—the whole family went. Unlike today, our parents weren't running a bus service to take each one of us wherever we wanted to go. I had little interest in playing sports and even less interest in watching my younger brother do it, so when I was dragged along to his football or baseball games, I took my sketch pad and pencil and found something to draw.

While the rest of the family watched my brother compete, I would search for abandoned houses along the side of the field. Returning on several occasions, I'd redraw the same house from different perspectives: as it looked that day, as a neoclassical structure, as it may have looked when it was built in the 1920s. There is no doubt that I can trace my love of architecture back to those days of finding run-down structures and reinventing them in my drawings.

Although home rehabilitation was not yet popular, I had already been rescuing houses on paper when I was in elementary school. This artistic focus made me a bit of an oddity. Very few boys were interested in art or design even though most of the architects, builders, and advertising executives at the time were men. Whether I knew it or not, my early understanding of where I wanted to go in life gave me confidence to connect with a larger group of kids and I found ways to fit in. I wasn't an outsider and I wasn't bullied. But I was still different.

In fifth or sixth grade, I began using my developing skills to help those around me. Since my parents were working, I often spent summer days with my grandmother who wanted to update her 1950s porch. As we discussed her rehab plan, I realized that Grandmom couldn't see what I visualized. But when I drew the design for her in 3-D, the concept came to life and she understood. That was when it dawned on me that other people don't view things the way I do. When I consider an idea, I can see everything three dimensionally without the encumbrances of reality. I picture things the way my mind's eye would *like* them to be, making it easy for me to perceive the potential in homes I encounter today. I walk through houses that are in deplorable condition and look beyond the problems to see the end result.

My son is now 13, and it has occurred to me that I began drawing house plans long before I was his age. Back then, my role model was Mike Brady and, in my mind, every design started with the asymmetrical sloped-roof, 70s-style contemporary featured at the start of each *Brady Bunch* episode. Given my limited exposure to architecture, I collected marketing packets from local builders and used a lead pencil and T-square to design my own subdivisions on vellum.

Toys

Today, when I need inspiration, I don't have to look far. It's all there on a shelf in my office: Life-Like Trains, Plasticville towns, countless erector sets, and models of iconic buildings. These collections opened my mind as a kid and they still motivate me today.

Toys, yes, but these objects of childhood were so much more. Lincoln Logs and erector sets required a kid like me to think. Although the sizes, shapes, and colors of available materials were limited, I managed to create new structures day after day. In the early 1970s, an expanded erector set emerged, with plastic girders, panels, beams, and posts. While only rectangular structures could be built, it was the front panel that made each design unique. Some looked like modern glass façades for a skyscraper while others had the brick texture of an office or the simulated wood siding of a home. By snapping on windows, doors, and other features, I could create anything I imagined. Without knowing it, I was learning how to work within constraints while testing designs for balance, counterweights, and overhangs.

Model trains provided another outlet. On a 10x8 board, my father built a track with two ovals and several offshoots, but it wasn't the engine or a railroad car that grabbed my attention. I was enthralled with the design and layout of the entire world I could build *around* the trains. The landscaping, parking lots, lighting, houses—and especially the control board—brought the scene to life. There was nothing like the smell of a sparking wire and the challenge to discover its cause. I'd lie under the track and work on the wiring for hours, shocking myself so many times that I'm amazed I can still speak today—or control my bladder. That track was an unplanned lesson in electricity.

As I got older, I collected all kinds of models and I still seek them out in antique stores. Many are plastic spinoffs of recognizable iconic buildings, restaurants, or hotels such as Howard Johnson, 7-Eleven, Tastee Freez, or McDonald's. With so many available options, an entire suburban city quickly comes to life.

Today's construction toys have continued along a different route. While LEGOs are still popular, computer games such as Minecraft provide a new way for kids to design block structures, build empires, and save their creations. Many of these structures defy worldly logic and disregard the laws of gravity—and kids like my son mostly enjoy slaughtering sheep and escaping ghostly escapades—but it's a new way to think creatively.

Bulletin Boards

Throughout elementary school, I spent most of my time drawing and building things, so thank goodness for my sixth-grade teacher, Miss Smorada. She managed to impart the things I needed to know without overburdening me with other nonsense that made its way into the curriculum. Miss Smorada realized that she couldn't press everyone into the same cookie-cutter mold. In fact, my future career had everything to do with the fact that she recognized my oddly-artistic-tied-to-naturally-mechanical abilities. By letting me do and be who I was, Miss Smorada freed me to be creative. This brings me to a story about bulletin boards.

Everyone remembers this menagerie of corrugated paper, glitter, cutout letters, and whatever else could be pinned, taped, glued, stapled, or thumbtacked to a corkboard wall. Whether teachers admit it or not, bulletin boards are competitive playing fields, signaling greatness or mediocrity. That rectangular, flat plane was the arena where I excelled at transforming a one-dimensional space into anything I wanted it to be.

After conjuring up an idea, Miss Smorada would turn me loose on a project and I'd run with it. I developed the theme, created a format, and translated it into shapes, designs, and backgrounds framed in a flat, yet dimensional, world. In Miss Smorada's class, no board was off limits—including the thin sliver of cork that ran above the chalkboard and around the room.

I loved those damn boards! There was nothing better than attacking a rectangular field with endless combinations of materials, tools, and construction methods. Best of all, Miss Smorada wanted to advertise something different every month, so my creations multiplied. Soon, other teachers were vying for my talents, "hiring" me to bring their visions to life. At the height of my bulletin board career, I was responsible for the fourth-, fifth-, and sixth-grade classes, the library, and the connecting hallway.

Yet, this story isn't really about bulletin boards at all. It's about power. Having the flexibility to do what I wanted provided my first glimpse at independence, creativity, and control. Through the unlikely vehicle of a bulletin board, I communicated confidence to teachers who soon relied on me for other responsibilities. The hardest part about moving on to junior high was walking away from the artistic arena I had built and the control and recognition it provided.

This wasn't merely an outlet; it was the foundation of something more. In fact, I can trace my 30-year career in department store merchandising back to my first bulletin board.

Treasures

Perhaps it was confidence—or more likely my developing ego—that kept me on track at school. I quickly learned that when you create things and put them out there for people to look at and give opinions on, you better have an ego. It might determine your position in life, where you go, or how you get there.

Although I could have become a latent starving artist, that's not who I was. I tried oil painting—of solid structures, buildings, and such—but I was always searching for the purpose beyond the drawings. For me, art wasn't the end. It was the *beginning*. Art was the vehicle that would get me where I was going.

My father built my first drafting table, complete with a square that rode across the surface on pulleys. Large and heavy, it took up my entire room, so we moved it to the basement. Along with the table, Dad passed along a drawing kit and vellum paper to get me started.

These tools were treasures: a metal pencil holder, pieces of lead marked with numbers for different line weights, compasses, spacers, smaller edges, and lead sharpeners. All of this was tucked into a leather pouch lined with velvet. I remember the feel and smell of the lead, the scraping sound of graphite on paper, and the crisp vellum rustling across the drawing board. These tools left such an impression on me that later in life I incorporated them into my tattoos, some of which are featured in the section headers of this book.

Drafting is an art, and I valued the tools that made it happen. It's hard to understand unless you've experienced this yourself, but there was nothing like the feel and appearance of those architectural tools and the splendid case that held them. Artifacts of another age, today their equivalents can only be found in antique stores.

Using these tools helped me discover an interest in the mechanical side of drawing and the fulfillment that comes from committing ideas to paper. With an increased exposure to architecture, my designs evolved and I began to understand that a passion was developing, although I was not sure where it was leading.

CHAPTER 3

Getting Schooled

Back when middle schools were still junior highs for seventh, eighth and ninth graders, I went to Surrattsville Junior High School. My parents got divorced after I finished sixth grade, so while other kids were making the school transition and enduring the horrors of puberty, I was doing that with the added challenge of a fluctuating family life. My mother had a new boyfriend who would soon become my stepfather, and even though he had his own house, he spent a lot of time living in ours. Change was everywhere—at home, at school, in the mirror.

But change turned out to be okay. Junior high meant more freedom to sign up for classes I was interested in, allowing me to add art to my curriculum. Just as I settled into a routine, things changed again when my mother announced that we were moving to southern Maryland. Saying good-bye to my lifelong friends, I dreaded the thought of starting over with unknown people. To make matters worse, I was dropped into an academic environment that was now called middle school with grades six, seven, and eight. The abrupt adjustment was like being held back once again. I signed up for art and drawing, but since many of my new friends at Margaret Brent Middle School had taken these classes the year before, it felt like a repeat of my second-grade experience.

As a quiet kid trying to find my way in a new place, I eventually learned that change can be a marvelous thing. To survive my frustration with home and school, I developed a solid group of friends who pushed me out of my shell. Stepping beyond my comfort zone, I became more involved in activities than before. It was my first taste of independence.

Inside the Box

As a result of my advanced drawing capabilities, I connected with the art teacher who taught me to bring my drawings to life. She was initially frustrated at my insistence on staying within an artistic box, focusing all my drawings on the buildings, houses, and scenery that interested me. Halfway through the year, my teacher realized how much I had invested in art and perhaps she even understood the role it would play in my future. From then on, she let off the gas and stopped forcing me to draw hands and humans.

With an increased attention on drawing buildings and the settings around them, I was determined to elevate flat structures by using a variety of shading techniques to give them personality and life. There were no computers at the time, so everything was created with pencils, pens, paper, markers, brushes, and paint. Driven to tell the story of each house, I used my new-found techniques to draw out its character. By eighth grade, I began to push the limits, depicting images other people could easily relate to. I entered art contests at county fairs and won ribbons that boosted my confidence, including a competition for the school yearbook cover. My drawing of a coat of arms is forever memorialized on the front of a 1970s-era Panther Postscript, complete with the school logo. These artistic achievements increased my standing with new friends, faculty, and people I didn't even know. In the midst of it all, independence was transitioning to leadership.

In art class, I began to learn how to communicate the house stories that still drive me today. I'm not talking about cookie-cutter designs with production features and lookalike façades. I'm compelled to tell the stories of desperate houses that need love and attention, of older residences that are different in a wonderful sort of way. Back then, the stories came out in my drawings. Today, my rehabs tell the tales.

Calculations

Architecture may be best described as calculated art, and that's where math comes in. Remember back in math class when you wondered if you'd ever use the stuff they were packing into your brain? Turns out, story problems are an everyday occurrence in the rehab business. That's why I owe a debt of gratitude to Mr. Baker. Here's how that story played out.

I left middle school as a B-C student, mainly because my grades reflected my level of interest in a particular subject and the classes I liked were few and far between. Yet, realizing that our family didn't have unlimited funds, I knew a scholarship might be my only ticket to college. I entered my freshman year with a determination to use academics, activities, and a steady group of friends to get me where I needed to go. I knew that math would be instrumental in my pursuit of an architectural career, but ninth grade algebra was tricky for me. When I found myself barely squeaking by with a D, I did the only thing I could think of at the time.

I asked the teacher for help.

Fortunately, Mr. Baker understood that I had a different way of learning. By taking the time to connect with me, he changed the way I looked at math. Each day after school, I did my homework in Mr. Baker's classroom while he graded papers or prepped for the next day. As we worked together, he managed to wrap my head around each concept by explaining the mechanics involved. He realized that memorizing formulas was not going to work for me. I needed logic. And once I understood the reasoning, it never left me.

I excelled at math because Mr. Baker translated concepts for me in a way that a book or memorization didn't. When I could see the formula functionally in my head, I understood it. Everything came together— like when you realize you've been looking at something backwards, or when I could truly see for the first time with the help of glasses. On a foundation of logic, I was easily able to build through each level of math: algebra, geometry, calculus, and trigonometry. When the parts came together for me, everything was a piece of cake. After completing all my high school requirements, I transferred to the community college for math during my senior year. It is incredible how things make sense when you understand the logic. I owe it all to Mr. Baker.

This experience was invaluable because I use math every day to save time, money, and heartache. Here's a fictional story that illustrates my point. Let's say a rehabber named Rob is thinking about buying a townhouse to renovate and sell. Having done the research, he's calculated the resale value at $200,000. As a responsible investor, Rob is not willing to purchase the townhouse for more than 50% of what he can sell it for later, so he needs to buy it at or below $100,000. He plans to spend another $50,000 rehabbing the house, bringing his projected initial investment to $150,000.

Before moving on with the project, Rob has a lot to consider. Tying up money over time costs money, and Rob knows that the timeline from purchase to sale will be much longer than the actual rehab schedule. His money will be locked in for the duration but it won't benefit Rob until the end. That means he won't see a penny of profit or repayment until the property sells.

Rob realizes that he can lose money—in fact, he *will* lose money—in this business. It's impossible that every project will sell for exactly what he needs, or that every budget will work, or that every potential problem will be avoided. Rob creates an excel spreadsheet that considers every aspect of the project, understanding that the rehab business doesn't work unless everyone involved makes money. Rob can't expect to pile up cash while he nickels and dimes everyone else. His contractors would walk, his vendors wouldn't work with him, and his network of trusted professionals would become very thin.

Now let's think for a minute about what would happen if Rob invested his money instead of exerting time, effort, and cash into a risky rehab project. As a smart guy, Rob wouldn't leave his cash in a savings account where it might make a ridiculous 1.3% interest. He'd allocate it to stocks or other sources that would earn at least 4% to 7%. Let's agree that if Rob invested his money he could make around 5%. At that rate, what is Rob's break-even point on his $150,000 investment?

Right. It's $7,500. File that number away. We'll be using it later.

Here's where the plot thickens in our story problem. Rob needs to factor in a whole slew of expenses, including transfer taxes, recording fees, settlement charges, utility reconciliations, water bills, and a multitude of other things that come into play. Given all the front-end requirements, he's learned to set aside about $5,000 on the settlement sheet, also known as the HUD-1.

Now let's talk about back-end costs. Rob and his Realtor have decided on a 5% sales commission, tying up another $10,000 and bringing the total to $165,000. On top of that, he'll deal with recordation, taxes, and more, so he's adding in $5,000 for miscellaneous fees, upping the overall amount to $170,000.

Keep in mind that during this time, Rob's money still isn't working for him. Let's say it takes Rob a year from the time he purchases the property, completes the rehab, and sells it. Now he has to figure in his $7,500 interest, bringing the break-even point to $177,500. That's if everything goes along as planned with no surprises. Trust me, surprises happen.

Now Rob is sitting at $177,500 and hoping to sell the rehabbed townhouse that he's put his heart and soul into for at least $200,000, netting a profit of $22,500. But he hasn't negotiated the deal yet—and buyers always want to feel like they get a bargain. A few of Rob's projects have been so desirable that people paid full price and closed quickly without asking for anything. No closing help, no price adjustment, no haggling. He knows those deals are rare because buyers almost always negotiate. So Rob allows $10,000 of wiggle room.

This is where the math gets fun. Not only will the buyers offer Rob $5,000 less than the list price; they'll ask him to pay part of their closing costs, too. Experienced rehabbers always need to consider the economics of the project at hand. In Rob's market, the $200,000 range means he'll be dealing with many value-conscious buyers who use FHA or VA financing. If they offer Rob $195,000 and require closing cost assistance of $5,000 for the beautiful house that he spent nine months rehabbing and three months marketing, Rob might feel like he needs to take it. That's $5,000 off the price and another $5,000 in closing costs, meaning that his negotiated deal at the settlement table is going to start out at a $190,000—not $200,000.

Remember, Rob needs $177,500 just to break even.

In this case, Rob would be left with $12,500 for all the late evenings, money spent, and lost time with family. Rob is not paying himself a dime other than this $12,500, and he knows he could have earned more at a part-time job paying $10 per hour. He has done nothing other than toil away his time on a hobby.

For a moment at the settlement table, Rob will be excited because he'll get a check to cover the $100,000 purchase price and the $50,000 that he spent on the renovation. His $150,000 is coming back to him, yes, but that's not profit. That just covers what he spent. When he gets the final check at settlement, he'll be very, very fortunate if he earns $10,000 of profit, let alone the $12,500 he calculated.

Let that sink in. Really think about Rob's story, understand it, and be careful. I have watched so many unsuspecting people get sucked into a flipping craze that will eventually go away. What if Rob's $150,000 investment was his nest egg? What if it had been his life savings and he tied it up for a year? With luck on his side, perhaps he broke even or made $10,000. He also might have lost it all. Sadly, I've seen many cases where hobby flippers tried to do this, and in the end, they couldn't afford to complete the job, selling the house at a loss just to unload it. Or they didn't think it through and lost everything to the bank, lender, or tax man.

Helping people avoid this calamity is one of the main reasons I wrote this book. Decide who you are and what you want to do. Is rehabbing your hobby, side job, or career? Prepare for the worst-case scenario and know where it could lead you in the most realistic terms. I'll fill you in on a little secret. The number that flashes on the screen at the end of the flipper shows on HGTV rarely includes all the hidden—but very real—costs. Like a lot of things on TV, it's based on theatrics and showmanship. That's okay because the show is fun to watch, provides ideas, and gets you thinking. It's all good.

But remember:
TV show = Not real. Scripted.
Math = Real. Logical.

Of course this story is about much more than math. Mr. Baker's story was, too. No doubt, he could have graded papers at home but he stayed after school and made a difference in my life. Teaching was his passion. I'm the beneficiary. For that, I'm grateful.

English, Spelling & Other Nonsense

At school, English and spelling were not my strong points because, unlike math, they involved nonsensical rules. Memorization wasn't the issue; I have almost a photographic memory when it comes to things that are logical. I excelled at Latin because it had a base structure I could build on, allowing me to apply the rules to every word. In Latin, the rules were clear and succinct—just like math.

But, through my logical lens, English was a struggle. Many of the rules were stupid, such as "i before e except sometimes when it doesn't suit our purpose." I grew up at a time when the successful men in my life had assistants or secretaries to handle such mundane things as taking notes and writing letters, so I was convinced I didn't really need this nonsense anyway. I was definitely wrong about that.

Getting Involved

By the time I was a freshman in high school, not only did I know *what* I wanted to do in life, I knew *how* I wanted to get there. With my sights focused on architecture, my heart was set on Rensselaer Polytechnic Institute (RPI) in New York. After telling everyone that RPI was where I would go to college, I didn't have a clue how I'd pay for it so I set out to improve my prospects for a scholarship. I joined clubs that allowed me to connect with ideas I was passionate about, identify areas where I could make a difference, and find ways to excel.

For starters, my friends and I joined Latin Club, which was a lot cooler than it sounds, mostly because of the toga parties. Tandy Corporation had just come out with the TRS-80, and our school bought one so we started a computer club, too. Sitting in the science lab, learning to write text and simple BASIC programs, I remember thinking that the computer seemed like an oversized calculator. It was fun but would never catch on. Guess I missed the mark on that one, too.

Despite my lack of English skills, I became involved with the school newspaper. I loved the story perspective, digging into "the five Ws and an H" to discover who, what, when, where, why, and how. My favorite part was the layout process that included a lightbox, typesetting, and text. Arranging stories on the page was a natural progression from the bulletin boards I loved in elementary school. The paper was handcrafted every month and I was driven by the challenge of fitting blocks together to create something unique, useful, and cool.

Despite being uprooted midway through high school, I progressed from being a member of the newspaper staff to serving as editor-in-chief. At my new school, we didn't settle for complacency; we changed the paper's banner heads and layout, updated the theme, and made it more interesting and exciting. The real benefit was learning about drafting and using the tools of the newspaper trade—knives, glue, and pica tape—to create blocks and lines with different styles and sizes. Without the benefit of today's digital revisionist capabilities, it wasn't always perfect but we gave it our best effort before sending it off to the printer.

In seeking out activities, I was drawn to those that required creativity. I built sets for plays and was involved with designing every dance, party, or prom. In high demand, I came up with drawings, developed plans, and ran the groups. With my loyal band of workers, we could build just about anything: homecoming floats, theater stages, and party decorations. It was a team effort; I generated the design and then it was all hands on deck. It's the same with my crews today. They *get* me. As we approach each project, my teams know I'm going to take it to the next level and bring them right along with me. They might be surprised to learn that this all started with homecoming floats and class plays.

Beyond the clubs, I was interested in student government, serving as class vice president during my first two years of high school. As a sophomore, I became president of student government, a role that provided me with a direct connection to everything going on with classmates and faculty. My leadership skills developed as I gave speeches and handled other responsibilities. By establishing a comfort level with public speaking at an early age, I learned to express myself through my own voice in a natural way. Although I didn't know its impact at the time, this skill opened doors throughout my career.

Fitting In

Don't get me wrong. I wasn't an overly popular kid, because the activities I was involved with were unconventional. People noticed me, but I wasn't accepted for the reasons most kids were, like sports and social status. I was somewhere in the middle, creating a niche of my own that seemed to sit alright with 80% of the people around me. I was a chameleon that fit in with any group at any given time. In high school, adaptability was a survival technique; in the years to come, it enabled my journey.

Focused on my Rensselaer goal, I was determined to get a school letter to add to my resume. This proved to be a challenge because the athletic department was extremely territorial about handing out letters, even to students like me who were involved in a ridiculously high number of school activities. I understood the concept of earning letters, but why only sports? To me, the value of a letter was related to school pride, a work ethic, and the accomplishment of goals.

In my student government role, I took on the uphill battle of trying to add academics and activities to the lettering criteria. I'll admit this was because I was a crappy tennis player and even worse in golf, the only two sports I had a prayer of competing in. The athletic department didn't relent on the lettering criteria so I played tennis and golf just well enough to get my letter. Once I earned it, I could add pins for other things, such as president of student government, editor-in-chief of the newspaper, and various class officer roles.

Letters and pins didn't mean nearly as much as what it took to earn them. While I was coming of age, things were coming together: the ability to lead, an eagerness to learn, a passion for art, a vision for creating something unique. These building blocks were leading me to something more.

Coming of Age

Around this time, I switched households and moved in with my dad, which required a transfer to McDonough High School in Charles County. Before changing schools, I convinced my parents to let me finish the semester at Chopticon, where I was involved in student government and other clubs. Thankfully, I found a teacher who was willing to drive me back and forth each day from my dad's house.

In late spring, I learned about a summer program led by our biology teacher. With a focus on exploring the Chesapeake Bay ecosystems at the farthest tip of St. Mary's County, the program had a side project that involved renovating a waterfront bungalow. It was another seemingly ordinary story that turned out to be extraordinary.

Due to its water-oriented location, the project's county-owned property in southern Maryland was often used for summer youth camps and recreational programs. It was a beautiful piece of land that included a center-stair colonial mansion, a bungalow, and outbuildings that dated back to the early 1800s. In a state of disrepair, the bungalow was secluded from the main estate home, becoming the target of frequent vandalism. With funding in place, it was the county's goal to renovate the bungalow for a local police officer who would live there and keep an eye on the place. Our teacher would assemble the adolescent crew to make it happen.

Only a handful of students were selected for this unique task and I was lucky to be one. To qualify, I had to maintain a specified GPA, pass a test, and get the blessings of the teacher and my parents. Despite a lack of interest in biology, my overall grades helped me win over the teacher, and my parents were on board, too, if I could find transportation. Since the other kids in the program lived near the school, they would ride to the site with the teacher but my dad's house was located outside the district. Thanks to my student government connections, the school helped me develop a solution. In return for mowing and other maintenance, I could live in the on-site mansion for the duration of the summer program. Remember, I was 16 years old, didn't have a car, and had not seen the site before agreeing to this plan. Yet, as a typical teenager, I thought nothing could be cooler than living on my own and working on a project that interested me. With my usual finagling, I convinced my parents to support my scheme and pack up the stuff I'd need to survive on my own for six weeks. On the Sunday before the program began, Dad and I set off for the 90-minute drive south.

The trip seemed to take us an eternity from home but I had no fear because I was headed to a summer of freedom. We drove through the marsh on a raised road, arriving just as the sun was setting over the bay. To say the property was secluded is an understatement; it was a stunning scene that belonged in *Gone with the Wind.* The house faced open water tinged with orange, yellow, and blue-black and its exterior was comprised of clapboard, brick, and stucco with four chimneys rising above the roof. In the front, Palladian windows and porch remnants overlooked the water while the back was flanked by a low-lying marsh.

A key to the back door had been mailed to me along with instructions so I let myself in and Dad followed. I quickly noticed that the interior had been painted a glossy mint green color likely left over from the last school renovation. Elegant woodwork and classic fixtures had been left in a state of disrepair under 10-foot ceilings, giving the once-dignified home an air of suspended animation.

One wing of the house contained a kitchen with an industrial sink, stainless steel refrigerators, and a commercial oven; all appeared to be recently added but rarely used. A back staircase provided a servant access that had long ago become obsolete. Moving farther inside, we discovered that the formal living and dining areas had been retrofitted as classrooms with desk-chair combinations, shelves, microscopes, and file cabinets. In addition, we found lines of chairs in a ballroom-style space that spanned the width of the house, complete with a magnificent fireplace and ample windows. Behind the main stairs, a hallway connected all the rooms, including a bathroom and an office where I found the only phone in the house.

The spacious upper level had approximately nine bedrooms and three bathrooms, although only one had actual fixtures, set in old black and white tile. Glancing around the house, we discovered that there were no drapes, cushions, or standard furniture other than some miscellaneous pieces in two of the bedrooms. There, we found a prison-style bed, a small, industrial file cabinet, and a random dresser. It was obvious that the gorgeous estate had bid farewell to its best days.

After exploring my home-away-from-home and choosing one of the back bedrooms that faced the swamp, I helped Dad carry my things inside. The bedroom selection had been easy since it was the only one with a dresser, and the bathroom was right next door. Setup was quick; I used the file cabinet as a nightstand, grabbed a lamp from the first-floor office, and unpacked my clothes. After Dad and I put the groceries away and located the lawn mower in the boat house, he said goodbye and I was on my own.

I was extremely excited to be by myself. The sun had not yet set and the sky was still putting on a dramatic show. I lingered on the beach near the boathouse until dark. Heading for the house, I realized that not only was it dark, it was pitch black, and I couldn't see my hand in front of my face. Thank God I had left a few lights on in the house so I could find my way back. Shuffling along the path, I'll admit to being a little creeped out when the marsh came alive with the deafening sounds of frogs and bugs.

More ominous noises met me when I entered the house. With no drapes or cushions to absorb the noise, the wooden floors and painted walls created echoes all around. Every sound was amplified. Locking all the windows and doors on the main floor, I tried to calm my nerves.

Upstairs in my room, there were new sounds. Open windows on the second floor ushered in a welcome bay breeze along with unnerving noises as old trim creaked and doors slammed shut. With many of the windows stuck or malfunctioning, I was at the mercy of the randomly located ones that worked. Fortunately, the window in my room functioned well and had a screen, so at about 10:00, I opened it, popped a cassette tape into my 1980s-style boom box and settled in for the night. Switching to the radio, I discovered that the only available channel was a classical music station I later grew to love. After learning everything I could about classical music that summer, I would blast that station in the evenings until it reverberated through the house. In fact, I later came to appreciate all the sounds associated with the mansion, inside and out.

But first I had to survive my first night. After a trip to the bathroom, I turned off the lights and music, realizing that I was truly alone a mile and a half from the main road in a dark, creepy swamp. Thinking about the fact that the only phone was in the first-floor office, I worked myself into a panic attack before managing to fall asleep. Awaking the next morning with more confidence, I was determined to make it on my own.

Soon after dawn, our teacher arrived in a van with the other students, about seven of us in all. Our teacher explained that the first half of our day would be devoted to biology, with the remainder focused on rehabbing the house. I don't remember learning much about the bay and marshes other than appreciating their beauty during impressive sunsets and storms. Yet, studying the critters that inhabited the marshes made them less intimidating, and I began to hear the sounds as music rather than eerie cries. As it turned out, there were no swamp monsters.

The main house was still being used for summer camp programs and was full of activity. Most days, I woke early to the sounds of camp counselors setting up programs for elementary-aged kids who thought it was cool that I lived there. In fact, they believed I was the generous homeowner, letting them use my house for their camp. They loved jumping up and down on my bed to wake me up in the morning, and it was not uncommon for twenty kids to be running up and down the steps at any given time. As the day ended, we often played kickball before they left me alone to my quiet evenings.

My favorite part of the day was the afternoon house renovation. I remember the first time we laid eyes on the little bungalow. Covered in trees and a long walk from the boathouse, it remained undiscovered until our teacher took us there. The tiny, beige structure had a window-filled porch that faced the bay and a modest interior consisting of a kitchen, eating area, bathroom, and some bedrooms. Old and dilapidated, part of the bungalow's ceiling had caved in, and there were moldy smells, broken glass, peeling wallpaper, and rotten sashes. Given my limited knowledge of homes at the time, my first thought was that we should tear it down and build something new. I remember thinking, "there is no way to save this, no way to bring it back." Yet, since this remodel was paying for our summer, we didn't have a choice. We were going to do it.

The first thing we learned was that our teacher was no more experienced than we were in rehab, so the house renovation was in the hands of a biology teacher/handyman and a team of adolescents. Believe it or not, this was a good thing, because we took pride in what we were doing and we were willing to learn along the way. With no Google search available, we were guided by stacks of books—most of which I still own—explaining the principles of plumbing, electricity, drywall, and more.

We started by pulling away old materials to uncover the bungalow's impact from time, weather, and neglect. They don't teach you this on TV, but demo day isn't really about haphazardly knocking holes in walls. It's more like being a surgeon. There are all kinds of things inside the walls—such as plumbing, wiring, ductwork, and structural components—that need to be identified before you start swinging a sledge hammer. With each careful slice, you discover details worth keeping, materials that could harm you, and ways to minimize future repairs. Instead of tearing into the job with reckless abandon, we painstakingly removed old siding and shingles so we only replaced those that were rotten or broken.

After the first week of surgically disassembling the house, a different bungalow began to emerge. With the old windows, doors, shingles, and other replaceable components stripped away, we saw through to the underlying structure. Like the skeleton of someone who had become old and wrinkled, the home's bones didn't show the same age as the exterior parts that had weathered life. When we pulled all that away, the structure looked solid and ready for a new generation of systems and skin.

The do-it-yourself craze had not yet spawned big box hardware stores, so we sourced our supplies from lumber yards and specialty shops that maintained minimal on-site stock. Whether it was a building component or decorative element, we had to endure the time-consuming process of researching each item, placing an order, waiting for it to come in, and finally picking it up. We quickly learned the value of a well-organized plan.

Although I didn't know any of my fellow workers before that summer—and we were an interesting mix of biology geeks and construction nerds—oddly enough, we all got along. Our teacher was learning, too, and beyond supervising, he helped us build strong relationships. He let us learn by doing and we became more efficient with every mistake we made. Acquiring knowledge in the field is different than studying in a classroom because the practical application provides instant evidence of both success and error.

One of our most memorable mistakes involved the ceiling in the large room at the back of the house. There is an art to hanging drywall and we were not sheetrock Picassos. Our best efforts to plaster, tape, and sand rarely produced smooth surfaces. As a result, we decided to use acoustical tiles for the ceiling, which could easily be stapled in place. Since we had not installed the proper sheathing, humidity caused the heavy material to break and drop to the floor. On our second go-round, we glued and stapled the tiles to a solid platform constructed of lightweight paneling. The interlocking pattern provided a textured look that was popular at the time. After trimming it out, we were happy with our second effort.

Working in teams, we changed windows and doors, installed sheetrock over plaster, refinished hardwood, and replaced roof shingles. With the home's electricity disconnected, we were limited to hand tools or those we could power with our on-site generator. Big jobs required the whole crew while smaller projects were handled in pairs with occasional checks from our teacher. Since my focus was on the kitchen and bathroom, I learned lifelong lessons about plumbing and electrical systems. It was my first introduction to plumbing vents—not just how to install them, but the fact that plumbing doesn't work without them.

Our time was limited by our summer schedule, so there was little opportunity for fun and games. We were on a mission to complete the project and I often stayed on the job long after the crew went home for the day. Immersed in the house until dark, I had a hard time maintaining my other on-site responsibilities such as mowing and weeding. With no summer camps on weekends, I worked on the bungalow around the clock.

The learning and renovating went on all summer as we discovered the right and wrong way to hang light fixtures, how to sweat pipes together, what you might find in an old-school fuse box, and the importance of grounding wires—after I blew myself off a ladder more than once. Could I have died on that project? Yes, probably three times. But I promise it was worth every risk. For the first time, I understood that things don't have to be perfect, they just have to be right.

I don't remember much about biology that summer—other than catching dragonflies and making glass slides for microscopes—but I will never forget turning that tired little bungalow into a home. It was a defining time when I was exactly where I needed to be. I often feel this way today. Sometimes life is about listening to what calls you, following what happens, and being unafraid to jump in. This was one of those rare, unexpected experiences that prepared me for what came next.

CHAPTER 4

What I Did for Half My Life

At 18, I was ready for change and, apparently, change was ready for me. On the home front, Mom and Dad were navigating the ebb and flow of divorce and new relationships. While adjusting to changes at home and school by immersing myself in activities, I earned the Senior Superlative as "the student who did the most for McDonough" despite the fact that I had only attended the school for a year and a half. I was older than most of my classmates and eager to be on my own, having worked three jobs since my sophomore year. Continuing my journey of independence, I moved into an apartment with friends in Waldorf where I could commute between work and school until graduation.

Perseverance

My college plans were becoming increasingly frustrating. Dad was strapped for cash and Mom had her hands full with my three siblings. How was I supposed to live on my own, eat, pay for a car, get insurance—and afford college? The need for a full-ride scholarship to Rensselaer was obvious, but with little time to invest in the process, my outlook was bleak. As a B student who was active in clubs but not athletic, the best I could hope for was a partial art scholarship. Foolishly thinking I could make enough money to pay for my college dream on my own, I worked part time throughout high school, starting with a job at Peebles department store in Waldorf. My hours were limited to 15 to 20 per week on evenings and weekends at a student wage that was less than $3.00 per hour.

Interestingly, of all the jobs I held, the one at Peebles figured the most in my future career. Starting out as a part-timer in the housekeeping department, I scrubbed bathrooms, vacuumed rugs, and changed light bulbs. While giving each of these tasks my all, I gravitated toward responsibilities that built on my strengths: controlling inventory, organizing the stock rooms, and fixing things. I glued delaminating countertops and replaced the screws on endless fixtures. Drawing on my childhood experiences, these roles came naturally to me.

My expertise with repairs led managers to send more projects my way. When a vendor sent a complex display to our store, I was tapped to assemble it. This was the turning point that propelled my housekeeping job into the vocation that would carry me through high school and into college. I was learning skills, developing a work ethic, and creating a foundation of trust. My boss saw beyond age and focused on my potential, giving me projects with increasing levels of importance. I painted offices and built displays. Best of all, he let me drive his red Fiero—which I thought was cool—to get it washed or have the oil changed.

After a short time at Peebles, I was placed in charge of the housekeeping crew. While still in high school, I had secured a management position with a flexible schedule—pretty amazing by today's standards. I soon gave up on Rensselaer and attended classes part time at the local community college. Paying the tuition myself, I seamlessly switched to full time after high school graduation. I muddled through core requirements while whetting my appetite for architecture with drafting courses.

To increase my income, I clocked additional hours at Doug's Hobby Shop in Waldorf. My dad and I had shopped at Doug's for years to support his model airplane hobby and buy the trains, buildings, plastic models, and art supplies that interested me.

This second job allowed me to add 15 to 20 hours of pay while working in a place I loved. My anal-retentive skill for arranging everything—army items, boats, ships, and vehicles of all types—made me well suited for the job. I soon took over the collection of trains and automobiles, spending hours organizing every make and model. My current knowledge of cars is based entirely on what I learned and visually retained at Doug's Hobby Shop. It was the same with train styles; I spent hours with them every week and could classify them all.

Given my experience at Peebles, I already understood the value of work performance that extends beyond a job description. At Doug's, I loved interacting with customers and helping kids conquer science projects. After convincing a student to share an idea, we'd brainstorm what to buy, which glue would work best, and how to incorporate the most interesting details. Inspired by my own art teacher, I encouraged creative thinking, recommending materials and specialty items that would make the project stand out.

In an effort to turn a collection of part-time jobs into full-time pay, I added late-night hours at the local skating rink. Arriving when the rink closed at 10:00 p.m., I'd clean the snack bar, vacuum the common area, mop the skate floor, and scrub the bathrooms. I can say from experience that cleaning bathrooms used by teenagers at a skating rink is very, very different than sprucing up the lavatories at Peebles. But I did it, prompting Skip, the manager, to increase my responsibilities. He relied on me to retile the arcade area, paint the lockers, rotate seasonal decorations, and revitalize the snack bar with an illuminated Coca-Cola wave.

As my working relationship with Skip developed over time, I became the assistant manager, running the snack bar, operating the skate room, remodeling the bathrooms, and even serving as an occasional DJ. I was an old soul; Skip trusted me to handle whatever was needed and he became my friend.

Like teachers, bosses can be pivotal. I've always been close to my managers because I believe that good relationships are the foundation for a successful work environment. Actually, it's more than that. Good relationships bring out the best in each one of us regardless of position. Some people call this brown-nosing; I call it networking. With this approach, I've learned and grown at every job. I carried Skip's lessons of trust and resourcefulness into my architectural career. Our friendship spanned decades and we're still there for each other today.

Opportunity

After graduating from high school, I focused on managing my housekeeping team at Peebles, juggling side jobs, and using the whole deal to achieve my college goal. Taking three classes each semester (which I did most of the eight years I was in college), I didn't have a lot of extra time on my hands. To accommodate school, I finally had to reallocate my schedule and give up the job at Doug's.

At Peebles, my responsibilities grew as I managed the crew, kept the books, oversaw deliveries, and handled special projects. My boss was ridiculously supportive, letting me design the schedule that fit my needs. While working my way through college, I discovered it was actually my *job* that was providing the most relevant education and opportunity.

The ensuing career I never imagined was launched by a staffing fluke at Peebles that required me to work the sales floor in housewares. Since microwave ovens and high-end Weber grills had just emerged on the retail scene, the store sent me to a class to learn more. New to the market, microwaves were an enigma. People thought the appliance cooked by magic which is no wonder because they were sold by a vendor called Magic Chef, which taught my class. In short order, the training dispelled the myths, streamlined the display process, and provided me with the logic behind the microwave magic.

I became a master at building vast microwave landscapes that spanned an entire row of the housewares department. In fact, I was so good that Magic Chef issued a silly award and recruited me to set up displays and market their products to other retailers. With my sights still set on school, I declined the offer due to its travel requirements, a scenario that was repeated when Weber made a similar proposal. Young and enthusiastic, I was a viable candidate for this type of role but unwilling to leave college and give up on my dream.

That's when a door opened—into the world of store displays.

I know what you're thinking: store displays are all about mannequins. That's what I thought, too. I'm not a fashionista, so I hadn't paid attention to store displays or the world of construction associated with them. I quickly learned that store displays require a dynamic workshop where kitchens are built, window exhibits are designed, and mannequin platforms are fabricated. With precision, valences are hung, materials are painted, and lettering is affixed to walls. Other than the building's structure and fixtures, everything visible in the store is created by the display department. Although I had never thought about this, a chance occurrence changed both my perspective and my path.

It started when an assistant resigned, leaving the manager, Mary, short staffed just as she was preparing for maternity leave. Until Mary returned, I was asked to step in, quickly discovering that I had a knack for crafting store displays. In many ways, I had been doing it my whole life.

I was enthralled. Managing the displays was a natural extension of my experiences with wood scraps, bulletin boards, and newspaper layouts. Store displays were dynamic, three-dimensional arenas where I could build almost anything I wanted. Before Mary left, I followed her lead, incorporating our ideas with funding from the corporate office. When Mary said we needed a *this* or a *that*, I'd head to the shop and transform wood, lights, and simulated foliage into a spring towel gazebo. Discovering that I excelled at making these whimsically-useful displays gave me the confidence I needed to run the department full time in her absence.

Don't get me wrong. During that time, I made a bazillion mistakes and produced some incredibly stupid stuff. The credit for accomplishments goes to Mary, a great teacher who became a lifelong friend. Without beating me down, she established an environment of trust, encouragement, and honesty. It was Mary who made me believe that mistakes and stupid stuff can become our best projects. Sometimes the things we don't mean to do are the things that end up being our greatest achievements. Perhaps that's my life story.

When Mary returned after maternity leave, I was in my sophomore year of college and relied on work to fund my classes. While the Peebles team appreciated my talent, their budget was too small for two managers. As a result, they encouraged me to accept a similar role at another store or move to the corporate office. Given my commitments to family, side jobs, and school, relocation wasn't in my plan.

Exploring other options, I answered an ad for an assistant display shop foreman at Woodward and Lothrop, also known as Woodies. The job involved managing materials, tools, and labor for one of their biggest department stores, allowing me to focus on design and construction while avoiding mannequins and other nonsense. Located near the D.C. line in Marlow Heights, Maryland, the store was a viable commute, only about twenty minutes from my home on Branch Avenue. When I received the job offer, it was hard to leave Peebles, but Mary helped me navigate the change and gain traction at my new job.

Before working at a large chain, I hadn't fully understood the diversity and creativity of the display shop teams that I came to know and appreciate as coworkers. I can say from experience that the movie *Mannequin* did a fine job of depicting the whole scene. Our projects were extremely structural, with a massive scope and scale. Bringing nine to fifteen windows alive for the Christmas season required months of preparation, nonstop construction, gallons of paint, hundreds of trees, endless strings of lights, and ongoing craziness. I loved every minute.

Within a year I was promoted to assistant manager at a major Woodies store in Tysons Corner, Virginia. The regional director later selected me for a training role at the main store in D.C., where I got my first real office and my career took off. Although it was years in the making, I finally received financial support for my education. In my new position, the company reimbursed 80% of my tuition and books as long as I maintained a B average, was on the Dean's List, and took classes that loosely related to my vocation. It served as the scholarship I always wanted, paying for about five of my eight years in college.

The rapid career advancement meant transferring my community college credits from Charles County to Prince George's to facilitate a more reasonable work commute. Staying in Maryland was important because my program was designed to culminate in a degree at the

University of Maryland's architectural school, which I had decided was a solid replacement for Rensselaer. My heart was set on it.

Side Work

As if going to school and working full time weren't enough, I always had a side project in the works to satisfy my interest in residential architecture. When my father updated his 1980s contemporary home, I designed and constructed a new full bath, free-standing garage, workshop, and second floor apartment. At my friend Rob's place, I added a pool pavilion and separate garage.

Over time, small projects grew into major endeavors. When my uncle's waterfront house in southern Maryland burned to the ground, I was recruited to rebuild it. Although county restrictions limited me to the shape of the original foundation walls, I could design to my heart's content within that footprint. I found the challenge inspiring. Like bulletin boards, the framework of my canvas was defined, and within that space I could incorporate the creative expression I was learning at work. To this day, we are still amazed at that waterfront house and how vastly different two structures can be, sitting on the exact same foundation.

Around that time, my sister, Jenni, was making her fortune as an east coast scrapbook queen, having developed her own line of papers and accessories. Her scrapbooking company became so successful that my brother-in-law, Jared, left his job to help her run it. Ahead of their time, the two of them planned a move to the emerging Nashville market, hiring me to craft their vision of an updated 1800s plantation house. For inspiration, they sent me a concept plan that we transformed into a gracious, three-story residence with a stacked, wraparound porch. True to its style, the design included a mansard roof, widow's walk, gas lights, plenty of French doors, and brick-arched porticos. With authentic details, it was a striking residence.

Similar to my building experiences throughout childhood, I learned something new with each project. In the process of helping family, friends, and their referrals, I wore a lot of hats: consultant, designer, general contractor, and laborer. While these side jobs didn't pay well in the monetary sense, they provided a lifetime of experience I wouldn't trade for the world.

A New Dimension

To accommodate my growing career, I finally trimmed my daytime college schedule and added night and weekend classes, carrying a heavier load during the summer months. With the onset of televised classes and cable TV access, the technological landscape at college was changing, and that convenience couldn't have come at a better time for me. I supplemented my curriculum by recording classes on my VCR and watching them after work. When concepts were confusing, I submitted questions to the professor via a call-in number. After mastering this technique, I expanded my online course load at the University of Maryland to expedite my college plan.

While I was making my way to the University of Maryland, computers were emerging in the classrooms. This was a radical change in an architectural world which had been built on a foundation of pencils, vellum, and mechanical tools. Although I understood both the manual and computer methodologies, I clung to my view of drafting as an art form by teaching a class for underclassmen.

Seeking to learn the early versions of AutoCAD, I found it difficult to relinquish the craftsmanship of physical drawing. I could relate to the program from a math perspective, using the digitizing board's X, Y, and Z axes I knew from algebra. With digitizing pen in hand, I tapped points on the graph-lined grid to communicate with the computer and create a three-dimensional drawing. The process was unbelievably cumbersome; tapping points to create lines took four times as long as drawing them on paper. As we navigated the technological changes, my classmates and I predicted that computers would never succeed in the drafting process.

During a typical class, it took so long for each image to render that after the points were selected, there was a 50-50 chance that the computer would crash before a drawing appeared. Frustrated, we spent the first half of class locating points for the drawing and the second half rendering the image. Always resourceful, we found ways to endure the ordeal. With precision timing, we'd hit the button to begin the rendering process, head to the pub, order fries and a beer, and hang out until the drawing materialized. Sometimes, our plan was successful. More often, we returned to learn that the computer had crashed and we had to repeat the entire process. It was a nightmare. I stuck with it because I understood that the computer's role in architecture was growing. I just didn't realize how much.

The computer's impact on campus continued to develop in a variety of ways. With AutoCAD still in its infancy, digital arts were growing and I was eager to learn. New programs and software such as Amiga enabled 3-D animation and artistic illustration using electronic pens and endless colors. Everything became faster, easier to revise, and a cinch to save. To remain relevant, I stayed engaged as new technologies emerged, learning the analytical side of programming before shifting to the artistic focus that interested me the most.

While my college pursuits had earned me an associate certification and other credentials, the computer's impact on the School of Architecture had made many of my previous classes irrelevant to the degree I sought. After amassing enough knowledge and logging sufficient time for a five-year architectural program, I was confronted with an abundance of new requirements. I tried testing out of basics, bypassing prerequisites, and taking more classes in an attempt to piece together a graduation scenario. Despite taking years of classes and being inducted into a national engineering honor society, it appeared that I might never get a piece of paper with a degree on it.

Career Growth

At work, I continued to excel at visual merchandising while learning the best ways to lead people and projects. Not expecting the job to grow into a career, I was pleasantly surprised when my experience resulted in an apprenticeship at the new corporate office just across the Potomac River in Alexandria, Virginia. There, the Woodies store planning department—an in-house version of the shop that would be farmed out today—was comprised of executives and staffers who created budgets, hired contractors, and managed tasks for rehabs and new construction throughout the chain. Powered by available capital, the pace was fast and furious. As an experienced draftsman who was learning the latest techniques in college, I helped to facilitate their transition from hand-drawn designs to computerized projects.

I loved store planning. Uniquely directed to the end customer, it was an interesting marriage of art and design. The role expanded my horizons and challenged my capabilities. Working to stay current on new materials, active vendors, and negotiation techniques, I began to value the computer as a vital tool for business and communication.

As my passion for the business was escalating, Woodies was purchased by The May Company, which had been buying up retailers such as Hecht's in our local market and Strawbridge's and Wannamaker's in Philadelphia. The acquisition prompted the painful process of displacing employees when duplicate stores in single markets were shut down or sold.

At the time, I was working as a visual manager in Annapolis. Amid the transition, I soon accepted an offer from Bloomingdale's in New York, plunging me into the retail fray between Manhattan and White Plains. Buoyed by lifelong experiences with change, I quickly adapted, teaching classes for new managers while directing merchandising for two stores near our home in Westchester. By then, most of the construction components of store planning were being contracted out, shifting my attention back to visual arts. Merchandising was key, with a focus on presenting the product, making it appealing, and using visual elements to communicate the benefits.

At this point, you might think I had it all: a career in Manhattan, a swanky house in Westchester, and a wife I loved. But, in nine short months, I was miserable. It wasn't the company or the job. New York was nice, but it never felt like home.

Relying on my network of trusted relationships, I reconnected with colleagues at The May Company who valued my work ethic and hired me as the visual merchandising coordinator for the men's and children's departments in their growing spectrum of 80 to 90 stores. Not only did the job provide me with a ticket back to Maryland, it evolved into a regional director of merchandising role that facilitated a more comfortable living environment for our family. As the youngest employee in a director position, I quickly fell into the stereotypical corporate web, lured by a salary that paid for things like cars and homes, while trapped in a spot where I was always hungry and wanting more—which is exactly where they wanted me.

The advanced skills I had acquired in AutoCAD continuously paved my path in merchandising. I went on to become a vice president, working in that role until the next inevitable takeover. Eventually, Federated Department Stores which owned Macy's purchased The May Company which owned everything else. In the midst of these changes, I was selected to oversee the planning, installations, and negotiations for vendor shops such as Polo, Nautica, and Tommy Hilfiger. These brands were featured on structures within our store and my department was in charge of it all, including design, construction, and purchasing.

This is when I finally realized that having a degree was no longer required for my career. At work, I had advanced to the level of vice president. Employers were mostly interested in computer skills and management abilities, and my experience ensured that I was up to date on that. After eight years of college, I finally let go of my quest for a paper degree.

Then, my job uprooted me again. This time, we settled in Alpharetta, Georgia, where I commuted to work in Atlanta until Macy's underwent severe cuts in capital. With the elimination of the Atlanta office, I was encouraged to connect with the New York team. It took me less than a New York minute to decide I wouldn't be going back there.

30 Years in the Works

This story has a happy ending. Time was on my side. Having been hired by Woodies way, way, way back when, I was now approaching my 30th anniversary in the business, placing me four years away from a fully-vested pension. The company was accommodating, reassigning me to manage the east coast's furniture division from an office near our home in Bel Air, Maryland. Managing store remodels and furniture updates took me from New York to Richmond and everywhere in between.

Instead of a happy ending, perhaps this story really has a happy *beginning*. When I hit the 30-year mark, it dawned on me that, after all those years, I had finally found my starting point. Three decades in retail had helped me discover the career I spent my entire life preparing for.

CHAPTER 5

Why Did I Wait 30 Years to Do This?

Today, people expect instant gratification. Post a picture on social media and humans around the globe immediately engage. Conduct an online job search and hundreds of candidates respond. Far different from this, my journey has been a long, winding path of childhood activities and work experiences. It was filled with accomplishments, mistakes, and do-overs. Along the way, I discovered that my formative years and professional experiences had been feeding my hunger for architecture without satisfying my appetite. I couldn't put my finger on it, but I knew something was missing.

My career journey seems to be scripted—in a wild sort of way—although I didn't understand that early on. After 30 years, I figured it out. Commercial buildings lack what I call "humanality," the combination of human characteristics and personality that can only be found in a house. Businesses and store displays are cost-effective theater sets designed to appeal to the masses. They are illusions. Residences are real. Homes are part of our communities and part of us, standing as unapologetic extensions of each and every owner. This realization not only differentiated my approach to residential renovation, it defined my career.

First and foremost, I am intrigued by the relationships between human beings and the homes they inhabit. People could easily live under tents or tarps. After all, it's just shelter, right? Not really. In many ways, a home is synonymous with the life within. People don't just own a home, it becomes their heart. In photos, the home is featured with family and friends—and perhaps a dog or cat—assembled right there on the front porch. Owners will decorate their homes for the holidays, reject hundreds of paint chips in search of the perfect room color, and care for physical misgivings over time. A home is vital to life.

While understanding this passion people have for homes, I think mine has always been greater than most. Architects and designers know what I'm talking about. Like a psychologist who brings out a person's true character or personality, an architect, a designer, or a rehabber sees beyond the brick and mortar to bring out the best a home can be. The more I've seen the architecture of bygone eras and witnessed the decline of past styles, the more I feel compelled to help these structures, keep them, and save them—from obscurity. People often feel this way about art or music. I am inspired by homes, and the intensity grows stronger with each one I encounter. Developing organically through time, this is a passion fueled by persistent questions. Why are there different architectural styles? How did necessity drive the height of a roof, the angle of a pitch, or the composition of exterior materials? Why have some building techniques changed while others remained the same? Why do people cling to relics of the past? Through the years and around the world, why has the residential home grown into a passionate extension of each family? How does a home represent the very fabric of life?

The House Listener

One of the hardest things for me to explain is how I listen to a house in order to save it. When it's right, a house speaks to me and I've already bought it in my head. I rescue houses that are more than shelters; they are places people fall in love with because of their character and functionality. It's my job to preserve or even elevate a house's dated style and classic features for a new generation of owners.

I don't buy the box, the plain Jane, unless I feel that there is more life inside, a truly compelling reason for someone to call it home.

Stress

This might sound easy, but things get in the way. For starters, I'm high-strung. I overthink things, worry about minutia, and replay decisions in my head. During my 30-year career in department stores, I'll confess that there were times when I needed medications to stay calm. Since leaving retail, I haven't had to endure an anxiety-related health issue. Now, as the sole proprietor of my company, I determine the schedules and the money and the pressures. I'm not saying it's been easy—or that I haven't spent millions of dollars. I still have plenty of stress, but it's no longer inside me. Now it's on the outside. The best way I can describe this is like wearing a suit. I can feel and see that the stress is there, but I determine how to wear it. This understanding of anxiety has changed my outlook on everything. Now, I'm in control.

Why did I wait to find this drive, this meaning, this happiness? Why does anyone wait to grab the thing in life that he or she is most passionate about? In my opinion, life is too short to waste your life doing things that are uninspiring. Take control and find happiness. For God's sake, I learned this in elementary school after conquering bulletin boards. Why did I forget that?

Fear

Here's the deal. We get forced into corners by a paycheck. Big companies know what they are doing when they increase our salaries, give us promotions, help us buy houses, award bonuses, and create joy in our lives. They do those things to keep us working, tie us down, and make us complacent. This isn't paranoia; it's just how things are.

Like most people, I work to make a living. I don't need to be a millionaire but I want to put food on the table, support my family, and take care of our house. For years, the fear of loss kept me nailed down to jobs I wasn't passionate about. It's not that my former bosses didn't take good care of me. There were great managers all along my career path who helped me grow. But fear kept me locked in place.

I was terrified of the unknown, afraid that I would not be successful, and scared that I might fail. Guess what? That's perfectly okay, because failure is part of life's formula. With the right perspective, failure is the ingredient that develops us into better people. I learned this from my biology teacher in southern Maryland and later from Mary at Peebles—and it is still true today. Making a few blunders helps us see what we're doing wrong—and sometimes that's the only way we learn how to do things right.

Don't let fear guide your life or you'll end up like me and wait until you're 50 to find the thing you were always meant to do. It's a hard, hard corner to turn. I reached that point after a long line of moves and changes and relocations that had nothing to do with what I wanted most out of life. When I was ultimately faced with the challenge of managing a career in New York from a home base in Maryland, it pushed me over the edge.

I knew I had to make a change right then—because I was finally scared to death.

Motivation

I'm still scared today, but it's different. Now, it's motivational fear. These nights, I lie awake at night because I'm excited about tomorrow. I wonder about whether to spend money, how to implement something new, or when to pull the trigger on a deal. I think, I think, I think. Now *I* make the decisions—not someone else. This motivates me to venture out of my comfort zone, past my fear, and beyond the control of a paycheck.

What drove me to walk away from a secure paycheck and the 30-year career I loved? I can sum it up in one word: control. I finally decided not to uproot my life or relocate my family again for the collection of a paycheck that left me feeling like something was missing. Now my days are fuller. I'm healthier and more productive, with power over my family time, my daily focus, and my future.

PART TWO

THE HARD PART

No one said this would be easy. Brain work is the hard work.

49

CHAPTER 6

Is It a Career or a Hobby?

If you're interested the rehabbing business, do yourself a favor before you dive in. Decide how you feel about what you are doing right now. Recognize what is happening around you, give yourself a nudge, and leave fear behind. *Take control.*

If you think you're ready for a change, do some research before you decide. Analyze the market, walk a few houses, test the waters, and ask some questions. Do you understand how to evaluate a house and truly hear what it is saying? Does your plan match your passion and direction? Do you want to rehab your own home, work on a few part-time projects, or build a successful business? Are your expectations realistic? Listen to yourself and understand the fit that is right for you. *Take your time.*

If you view rehabbing as a hobby, there's nothing wrong with using a little know-how to do something you love while maintaining your 9 to 5 job. Be prepared to work long hours that interfere with your current career for a minimal financial return. You'll be relying on contractors and vendors who operate in the same daily timeframe as your main job, so they won't be available when you call after hours. I'm not saying it's impossible to be a rehabber on the side. Pursue your passion if that's where it leads. Just understand it's hard work that can quickly devour a lot of cash. *Take care.*

If you decide to become a full-time rehabber, there is no get-rich-quick scheme, so don't walk out on your current career unless your heart is all in. Expecting easy money is the best way to fail miserably. You'll know it's right if you're realistic about your research, willing to develop a credible plan, and doing what feels natural. Otherwise, this is not the business for you. It has to come from the inside. *Take heart.*

CHAPTER 7

Getting Started:
Empty Your Wallet

Once you decide to seriously consider the rehab business, you're bound to have questions. Where do you start? How will you fund your projects? Who can help you? This chapter is filled with stress-relieving, face-saving, and maybe even life-changing things to know before you begin. I'll start with the basics.

Be honest with yourself. Accept the fact that you have a lot to learn. Experience makes all the difference and, by definition, you won't have that at the start. Depending on how you manage it, your budget can make or break a project. Upfront costs vary with the wind and financial bombshells come out of nowhere. *Be prepared.*

Put in the effort. In this business, perseverance can be your best friend. Early on, I enrolled in real estate certification classes although I had no intention of becoming a Realtor. I took the classes to hone my skills in marketing techniques, learn about contract negotiations, and gain access to property search resources. Look for these types of opportunities to gain a basic understanding of the industry before you find a real estate agent, seek funding, and begin looking at properties. *Proceed with knowledge.*

Think three-dimensionally. When funds are tight, understanding the hidden expenses becomes critical. No matter how much you think this business will cost, it will require even more. It can be disastrous if you're using your own money, especially if it is your entire nest egg. Utilizing someone else's money can be just as tragic when you don't know what you're doing. *Protect your investment.*

Don't put all your financial eggs in one basket. This secret seems obvious but is often missed. We learned an important lesson in 2006 when people dumped everything they had into real estate. Don't blindly follow the crowd and assume that good things will happen. Work hard to build multiple income streams that tie back to your business. While writing this book, I have a lot going on: I'm constructing a spec home for a local builder, selling three lots, and leasing vacation rentals in an ocean-front community. There are always more things I'm angling to do. These projects are bound to overlap, creating a tremendous demand for working capital. *Diversify.*

✱ ✱ ✱ ✱

Now, let's get into the details. At any given time, I might have millions of dollars tied up in real estate. The way I see it, half of that money is profit and payback, but most of it is not mine. It belongs to the long-term investors that allow me to make things happen. Those relationships didn't appear on my doorstep overnight; they are the result of time, effort, and even a little luck. Here are some tips to help you shape your mindset, avoid pitfalls, and build a successful network of funding sources.

Change your perspective on borrowing. Securing funding sources is hard, humbling work. Do some soul searching before you take the leap. If you're a person who refuses to borrow money from anyone, the rehabbing business isn't going to work for you unless you're independently wealthy. Keep in mind that most wealthy people utilized other people's money to get where they are today. You have to let go of that voice in your head that says borrowing money is bad. Borrowing money isn't bad. Borrowing money *poorly* is bad. Borrowing money without a plan to pay it back is bad. Smart borrowing makes the economy work.

Realize that it's not about giving or taking—it's about investing. The stock market provides valuable insight for understanding this process. In general, every publicly-held business of any scale has investors. Nine times out of ten, the originator of a company sold an idea to start a business. If you own stock, it is nothing more than an investment in an innovator's idea. That is every bit as risky as what we are talking about here. As the owner of your rehab company, you are building a stock portfolio and leveraging real estate notes against assets to create the cash equivalent and reserves you need to run the business.

Be confident. With this mindset, you can be assertive in selling yourself and your ideas to investors. There are plenty of investor sources out there, but be careful—many of them are one step above loan sharks. It's not like borrowing money from your mother, although your mother may be an investor. You're seeking qualified stakeholders and giving them an interest in your business. These investors will have a stake in real property—tangible assets—that they can fall back on should the investment go bad. With this in mind, settle into a comfort zone and develop a strong portfolio to sell yourself to the investors you desperately need.

Start with relationships you already have. You need hard money lenders (HMLs) to succeed in this business but it's a catch-22 because these investors won't work with you until you establish a track record. Relationships take time, and you won't have a lot of that at the start.

> **Mark-It: Family investors can be instrumental in helping you launch your business.**

Focus on existing friends or relatives, like your Uncle Paul, who has cash available for investment. Since he already knows you, Uncle Paul may be your best opportunity for hard money until you've established a portfolio.

Establish trusted relationships with hard money lenders. Once your company is off and running, you'll need a foundation of investors from whom you can repeatedly access money without undergoing a lengthy negotiation process. In the rehab business, building rapport is every bit as important as building structures. Talk to people. Listen. Learn everything you can about lending opportunities in your market.

Everything in real estate is negotiable. Each lender operates differently when it comes to assessing points, interest, and other fees. Don't be afraid to make requests, push back, and question rates. Over time, you'll learn to determine the overall viability of each deal and how often to go back to the well with the same lender.

> **Mark-It:** **While you may pay a given interest rate for short projects of a year or less, you should be able to negotiate a better percentage on long-term projects such as vacation rentals.**

Be flexible. Stay the course and do what's needed to fuel the engine at the beginning. If you're like most start-up rehabbers, you'll only have access to small increments of cash at first. You have to play the hand you're dealt. To make matters worse, it costs more to piece together a group of small loans—$25,000 here, $30,000 there, and $50,000 somewhere else—because you'll be paying interest and points for each transaction. Early on, there were times when I sold three stakes to come up with the money to make one project work, but it kept me in business. Since those loans were tied to the property, they were paid off at settlement along with the points and interest. Throughout the process, I learned to pay attention, be resourceful, and develop win-win scenarios.

> **Mark-It:** **When I was relying on a list of small investors, I realized it would be in everyone's best interest to form an investment group. I encouraged the investors to join together and create an LLC of pooled money from which I can now borrow larger lump sums. While costing me less in the long run, this scenario also expanded their opportunity as an investment firm with a growing client base.**

Plan ahead. While everyone likes to avoid risk, there is no such thing as a risk-free project. To get start-ups off the ground, some HMLs pool money from a variety of sources such as self-directed IRAs, cash in hand, funds sitting in low interest accounts, or assets tied up in the stock market. Such investors might enter into a contract at an 8% return for a 12-month term which is likely better than they would get elsewhere. To make a profit while covering costs and taxes, these HMLs then sell the pooled money to someone like me at 11% or 12% along with a few points. As your business becomes more established, you may benefit from reputable HMLs that provide these types of short-term loans. With proven track records and competitive interest rates, they can be a good source of money for your business.

Hang in there. The quest for financial backing can be difficult, even overwhelming at times. You need to present yourself as a strong cash buyer offering a quick settlement, but with unreliable funding, you may be unable to offer either on your early contracts. Prepare yourself for unavoidable disappointments that may result from weak offers with contingent financing.

Tread carefully with bank loans. As funding sources go, banks present a greater challenge because their loans are harder to come by and usually require you to personally qualify. This approach will be difficult unless you have a large line of credit or you plan to make rehabbing a hobby that involves just one project at a time. Even if you are able to establish an adequate line of credit, the qualification process will require you to be a co-signer on your own business loan, subjecting you to personal financial risk. In this case, if you are sued or lose a property, your personal credit and finances could be at stake. Similarly, some lenders may require a consent before judgment to guarantee that you will personally cover the funding if a deal goes sour. In an effort to keep your business as detached as possible from your personal funds and residence, this is why HMLs are often the quickest, most viable source of funding.

Reassess your funding sources. Having multiple lenders over time can be costly. I started my business with many small investors—like Uncle Paul—and worked to fine-tune this into a trusted network. As a rule of thumb, it is a good idea to pare down your smaller investors as your business progresses, but be true to those who were with you at the beginning.

Mark-It: Develop a trusted lending network—but don't dump Uncle Paul.

When you couldn't get money from the big guys, you relied on Uncle Paul's money. If Uncle Paul still likes being a part of what you're doing, don't turn him away because Joe-Big-Investor has opened a million-dollar line of credit for you on a phone call. Start losing some of the outside investors that are of less interest to you personally, but keep Uncle Paul. You'll be glad you did.

Take charge of cash and time. I can't overstate the value of having access to cash in this business. Distressed properties will come at you from every angle and you have to be ready. There are numerous cases where a bank owns a property, had a stake in it, or has taken it back. Perhaps an estate is in a situation where a quick sell is required because a foreclosure is imminent and the sale is needed to pay off the mortgage. Positioning yourself as a cash buyer on these contracts gives you leverage with the selling entity, whether it is Fannie Mae or an individual.

> **Mark-It**: **A nimble response rate will put you in the driver's seat. Your ability to write a contract as a cash deal that will settle within 30 days gives you a demonstrable advantage over a contingent competitor with a loan that has yet to be approved.**

Position yourself for success. After years of experience, I've created trusted relationships to ensure that I have $2 million to $3 million available to me in a moment's notice. Using my spreadsheet, I provide a prospectus on each deal, review the details in phone calls or emails, and get a verbal okay to move forward. The follow-up paperwork is minimal, and money can change hands immediately or at settlement. While it took years to establish these relationships, the availability of cash is a game-changer.

Beware of (some) loan brokers. Don't waste time and money on loan brokers who charge you a hefty fee to connect with lenders you could easily find yourself. With predatory intentions, some of these brokers will be on your tail as soon as you establish an LLC. Many require a signed contract entitling them to a 1% fee if you use anyone who happens to be on their lender list. If you decide to work with a loan broker, go in with your eyes open and remember that everything is negotiable.

> **Mark-It**: **To avoid an unnecessary financial burden, don't sign loan broker contracts; retain the flexibility to operate independently once you've established lender relationships of your own.**

Learn from my experience. As a long-term strategy, you'll be much happier if you avoid the middleman and establish direct relationships with your lenders. I'm not throwing all loan brokers under the bus, but I've learned to be cautious. One loan broker accepted money from me, never performed, and disappeared as soon as payment was rendered. Others complicated things so much that I couldn't make any deals work. Here's a real-life experience that may save you from the heartache and loss of money I endured.

> *In an effort to reverse a never-ending-cycle of rejected offers, I talked to everyone and investigated everything but I was searching in the dark. I had avoided loan brokers because I knew that most wouldn't negotiate a deal until I had a specific property under contract, which was totally backward because I couldn't get anything under contract without funding. Go figure.*
>
> *Then I was referred to a loan broker we'll call Betty. Her company sounded legit and she was recommended by a colleague, so what could go wrong? I dialed Betty's number and provided the details of a house I was trying to secure.*
>
> *In my desperation, I was determined to make the deal work with this broker. I rationalized that Betty would have access to a long list of lenders and would know how to navigate the varying parameters that complicated the process. I talked with Betty, gave her my information, and was encouraged when she said she could help me make the whole thing work.*
>
> *Then she mentioned her retainer, explaining that—like any attorney or accountant—she would require upfront funds until our relationship was established and we could move forward as partners on an invoice basis. Attorneys thrive on this model.*

Let's step back and examine what a loan broker really does. It's basically a sales role, compensated on commission. In Betty's case, the commission would be paid when she sold a loan and finalized a deal between a lender and a buyer like me. At that point, the loan broker, or middleman, earns the commission, typically 1% or more.

Keep in mind that the sale between the lender and buyer depends on the loan broker's ability to make it work. If it does, the loan broker gets paid, and if it doesn't, the broker shouldn't be paid. Just like a salesperson, when there is no sale, there is no commission. You need to understand this because if you don't—like I didn't at the beginning—you're likely to lose out big time.

If you treat a loan broker like an attorney or accountant, you might get sucked into paying a retainer or upfront fee that guarantees nothing. Brokers that insist on this scenario receive payment even if they don't find you a loan. In essence, that's a fee paid without services rendered.

Betty charged me an upfront fee of $2,300. To many in our business, that amount may sound small. When you are a fledgling rehabber, it is a decent chunk of change—especially if it yields nothing. Betty insisted that she wouldn't connect me to any lenders until she received the amount in full. What could I do?

Stupidly, I thought about it and then stupidly I forked out $2,300.

After Betty confirmed that she had received the money, she phoned me on two different occasions, referring me to an uninterested lender whose qualification parameters did not align with my situation. In other words, for a fee of $2,300, Betty merely provided me with contact information for a lender who had guidelines that didn't fit mine.

Remember, the whole reason I paid Betty was to connect me to a qualifying lender that matched my needs. In the ensuing weeks, I tried to contact her many times as I struggled to get my property under contract. Unable to close the deal, I was losing time and patience, trying to maintain my relationship with the bank and solidify the contract. Despite all my calls, Betty only contacted me one more time, leaving a message about her two-week vacation. Still I tried to reach her, even involving the colleague who provided the original recommendation. Finally, I gave up, concluding that I had been taken and my money had funded her vacation to Fiji.

The story doesn't end there. I desperately wanted to get that property under contract. After many sleepless nights, I woke up one morning totally frustrated, with this elusive property just beyond my grasp and another one in my sights. Realizing that my reliance on others had failed to ignite action, I decided to fuel the fire myself. In fact, I was determined to pour lighter fluid on my plan by dumping my hard-earned 401(k) into my business, 15% penalty and all. I rationalized that the money I'd be making would balance out the penalty so it wouldn't mean a loss over the long term. With no thanks to Betty or any other loan broker, that is exactly how I funded my first project. I didn't like it and it wasn't my first choice. But it was the only thing that made sense at the time. Thank God it worked.

It was a lesson learned. As a business owner who understands the concept of paying for services rendered, I would have gladly paid the full commission for a connection with a lender that matched my needs. Although that didn't happen in my case, you still have the opportunity to avoid this trap. Here's the takeaway: If someone works like a salesperson, and acts like a salesperson—and quacks like a salesperson—don't pay that person a retainer. A good loan broker will earn your money by making a deal between you and a qualified lender before expecting a penny. Pay the commission that is earned *after* the sale is made.

My story didn't end with a loan broker. In many ways, that's how it kept going.

CHAPTER 8

Setting Up a Business:
LLCs, INCs, EINs & Other Acronyms

When you're ready to get down to business, first you have to set it up. If you've decided to become a full-fledged rehabber, start by asking yourself what type of business you will be.

Limited Liability Company (LLC)

If you will be the sole proprietor without others on the payroll—which is probably the best way to begin—you're a good candidate for a Limited Liability Company (LLC). An LLC allows you to create business accounts, collect money, make expenditures, and have company assets that are not owned by you personally. This format provides valuable separation in your personal and business accounts to protect your private interests if, heaven forbid, your entity is sued, the market falls, properties don't sell, you're forced to take a loss, or you encounter some other calamity. Rehabbing is a risky, volatile adventure. Keep your personal and business accounts separate.

While creating an LLC seems daunting, it's actually quite simple. Like most things these days, it begins with the Internet. Decide on a company name, go online, complete the paperwork, set things up, pay your dues, and you're in business. As long as you create a basic company with no major complications, you won't need an attorney to do this. The online tools will walk you through it all.

As part of the setup process, you'll be assigned an Employer Identification Number (EIN), which is like having a social security number for your business. This number will be used to track transactions as you pay taxes, own property, and purchase goods and services. Your EIN number is easy to obtain for a small fee and it will become a critical component of your business, required by every lender, deed, and document filed under your company name. Over time, it will become as valuable to you from a business perspective as your social security number is for personal use.

With your company established, the next step is to create the Articles of Incorporation that will summarize how you will run your daily operation. Online platforms provide questions to guide you through the process. For example: Will you be the sole member? Is there a board? Your articles will establish the name of your company, specify who runs it, and outline how decisions are made when it comes to borrowing money. Lenders will rely on this information to understand your business and determine whether additional parties need to be included on their loans.

> **Mark-It: Your Articles of Incorporation are instrumental to future funding, so pay special attention to the details and be sure to refile when there are changes.**

As an LLC, you won't essentially hire employees; you'll create contractor relationships with workers and business owners. This means that individuals or companies providing services for your business will be recruited and paid with a signed business agreement that designates them as contractors of the LLC.

> **Mark-It: By compensating all your workers as contractors rather than employees, the LLC format allows you to maximize control and minimize liability.**

From a tax perspective, the LLC is handled like your personal records.

At year end, you'll document money paid for services performed, issuing 1099s as required by the IRS. Clearly defining procedures for your contractors will help you avoid the nonsense of cash-under-the-table deals. This doesn't mean you can never pay a contractor in cash. It just means that you and the contractor will report all expenses through proper channels.

Project-Specific LLCs

Many people in this business will create a separate LLC for each project and some lenders encourage this practice. Here's how it works. You purchase a house and set up an LLC under the name of that project. Why would you do this? Remember, an LLC is designed to limit liability. By nature, it ensures that your liability ends when the property closes.

In this case, when the settlement occurs, you have two options: 1) you can close the LLC, or 2) sell it to the buyer. If you choose to close the LLC when the property settles, it will end your involvement and store the LLC data under the property itself. From your buyer's perspective, this is like making a purchase from a store that goes out of business the same day. It's disconcerting because the buyer might want to discuss a follow-up issue with an entity that no longer exists. In today's real estate market, imagine what would happen if a large homebuilder disappeared as soon as a homeowner settled. Whether the buyer had a significant problem or just wanted to ask a question, no one would be there to respond.

The second option makes the transfer slightly cheaper since the buyer essentially purchases the LLC along with the liability at the time of closing. From the seller's perspective, it works no differently than the first option except that the liability falls to the buyer at settlement. The bottom line is that no one can come back to the original holder of the LLC.

In Maryland, a buyer doesn't have a legal right to hold the seller liable after closing anyway, because real estate is sold *as is*. A buyer would only have recourse if a specific warranty was provided or if the buyer could prove that the seller had personal knowledge of a latent defect. For example, if the seller were aware of mold in the attic and knowingly transferred the health risk to the buyer, the seller could be sued. With the burden of proof falling on the buyer's shoulders, the legal team would have to demonstrate that during the time the seller owned the house, a defect was discovered, not disclosed, and covered up or not dealt with at all. In addition to being almost impossible to prove on the buyer's end, pursuing this type of issue can take a toll on buyer-seller relationships and impose severe financial consequences.

> **Mark-It: While there may be a few specific scenarios that warrant the establishment of property-specific LLCs to separate funds or to manage rental properties, I recommend that you steer clear of this approach.**

The Value of a Brand

As your company grows and develops, handle your brand with care. Core values are fundamental to my business because I'm doing more than creating designs, processes, and structures. I'm building a brand that will be genuine, strong, and uniquely mine. A brand is valuable, yet fragile. In my case, it has taken years to build this business from a single note to a full crescendo. If maintaining my fragile, valuable brand means going back to service a property many times after I sell it, then that's exactly what I'll do. My reputation depends on it.

> **Mark-It: While laws are in place to protect people, I've learned that a moral compass is my best guide.**

By viewing each project on its own merits, I provide personalized service that transcends a standard warranty. I do what is needed before, during, and after the sale. I return calls, fix leaks, repair pipes, address issues I didn't come across in the past, and treat people fairly. I do all these things to make the buyer happy, and yes, to encourage a good review at the end of the day. As a company that sells multiple assets under one LLC, I'm open to scrutiny. People can post negative comments, give all kinds of feedback, and expose my business to unexpected risk. Rehabbers who set up individual LLCs for each property might limit their exposure to much of this scrutiny. But they will never build a brand.

My core values drive decisions. I've always had a clear vision of what

RR Projects and Design LLC will be and I don't stray from that purpose regardless of the pressure. Day in and day out, my company is synonymous with quality and state-of-the-art design as evidenced through the prism of my modern approach to properties. This adherence to principles isn't cheap or easy but it always opens doors. I advertise, sponsor teams, and get my logo in front of people so they understand what I do. Real estate agents, clients, and casual visitors who follow me on social media remember past experiences, know about my next project, and provide recommendations.

One of my biggest challenges is getting fellow professionals on board with my business concept, especially when it comes to work expectations. It is critical for contractors, agents, and inspectors to understand that working for me falls halfway between a high-end retailer and a flipper. This means I don't expect to pay retail price for products and services but I won't cut costs just to meet the bottom line.

> **Mark-It: The more I surround myself with partners who share my mindset, the stronger my business model becomes. This is how reputations are built and equipped to thrive.**

Writing this book is an important step in building my brand because accelerating my goals includes a responsibility to share what I've learned. If you want people to value your work, get out of your comfort zone and expose your company to critical review. This starts with taking the risk, putting yourself out there, and building a company under one LLC. You'll find this approach liberating, because it naturally leads you to do the right thing and make thoughtful decisions in each step of the process.

CHAPTER 9

Building a Team:
Contractors, Subcontractors & Sub-subcontractors

Once your business is up and running, assemble a team of reputable contractors you can relate to and rely on. I look for high performers who are as concerned about their reputations as I am about mine.

Build integrity. When considering a contractor to join my team, I conduct regular interviews just as I did when I recruited district managers in my department store days. The process allows me to evaluate a candidate's business strategy, portfolio of work, customer reviews, and colleague feedback.

> <u>Mark-It</u>: In some cases, I offer a test run on a small job so I can observe a prospective contractor in action.

In your hiring process, be wary of contractors who cut corners. This frustrating behavior seems to be ingrained in contractors who have considerable experience with flippers. Perhaps they are motivated to beat their original estimates, increase profits, or make up for lost ground. Whatever the reason, it's easy to spot this conduct once the contractor is on site. For example, you'll notice that one screw is consistently used for a job that clearly requires two. Of course, all contractors are not like this so it is your job to find the exceptions. Thankfully, many of the *one-screw* contractors are snatched up by competitors who care more about cheap prices than high-quality work.

Demand for high performers increases when the economy is booming, making it more difficult to find and afford the best contractors. During these times, steer clear of low-hanging fruit and don't be afraid to drop a worker who is cutting corners. Do everyone a favor, cut bait, and move on. With patience, you'll find and retain dedicated professionals whose goals align with yours.

> **Mark-It: You'll know you have the right person when your contractor forces you to do the right thing in a tough situation. That's integrity. Hang on to it.**

Communicate consistently. Once you've done the heavy lifting and assembled a solid team of contractors, the real work begins. Communicate your expectations and remain consistent in your messaging. If, at any point, you notice a do-it-on-the-cheap mentality, don't wait. Nip it in the bud before the behavior becomes a habit. By constantly communicating your *two-screw* expectations, you'll develop a team that requires less management and exhibits more responsibility. This process is like a daily dance of discovery and resolution.

> **Mark-It: My preferred contractors don't settle for mediocre work. They are partners I can count on to complete one task while fixing two more issues they notice along the way.**

If one of your contractors is employing low-performers, talk about the issues and explain the benefits of change. Be persistent until one of two things happens: 1) the work improves, or 2) the contractor brings in a new subcontractor. Communication is key, and without these conversations, things can quickly snowball out of control. This story illustrates the importance of communication.

> *I was renovating a bungalow that had classic, five-panel hardwood doors with ornamental ball tip hinges. The antique brass patina was buried in 90 years of daily use and paint splatters. I intended to keep the doors and*

hinges in the house, although both would need some TLC.

While the doors were being restored and sealed, I asked a subcontractor to carefully clean the hinges, explaining that, over time, each door and hinge had been twisted and worn together as a unit. To ensure that they remained aligned in their original positions after the restoration, I asked the subcontractor to clean the hinges individually before replacing them on each corresponding door. I emphasized the importance of ensuring that the hinges were installed in the exact locations where they were removed.

When the photographer arrived to take pictures of the finished house, she called to ask why all the doors were disconnected and leaning against the frames. After cancelling the photo session, I learned that the subcontractor had taken all the hinges to his home for the cleaning process which was not yet complete. Although he said he had marked them all, I knew it was unlikely that each hinge would be reunited with its associated door.

At this point, I hired another worker to put standard hinges on the doors (at an additional cost, of course) so I could have pictures taken and keep moving forward with the project. As it turned out, the new hinges fit nicely and looked fine, with all the doors in good working condition. I sent a text to the subcontractor who was cleaning the ball tip hinges, asking him to prepare them for storage so they could be used in another house.

Now that the new hinges were installed, I scheduled another photo shoot for the completed project. Again, I received a call saying that all the doors had been removed. My response of "Are you kidding me?" might have been embellished with a few additional words for emphasis. As it turned out, the original subcontractor had returned to school and a different worker was now involved. Knowing how much I liked the ball tip hinges, the new subcontractor decided—on his own—to replace them on the original doors instead of storing them for another job as planned.

Despite the subcontractor's best intention to please me, I now had doors and frames with additional holes, graphite stains on white trim, and missing hinges that needed to be addressed before I could schedule a third photo shoot.

Here's the point: Even when you think you are communicating, you need to communicate more. Contractors are a unique breed. They like to work independently and are determined to figure things out on their own. The problem is that their solutions sometimes have little to do with what the customer actually wants. In this case, I was the customer and communicating would have made all the difference.

Be strategic. Establish a business strategy that includes creating a realistic budget, recognizing quality work, and managing costs over time. Allocate the money required to do the job right even if it means finding ways to save costs in other areas.

> <u>Mark-It</u>: **Rewarding superior workmanship creates a cycle of excellence. Occasionally, I offer a bonus for every substantial defect a contractor identifies and fixes beyond the original scope of work.**

To avoid surprises and ensure consistent quality, create spreadsheets for each component of a job and compare costs across time and projects. For example, as I write this book, my paint number is $2.88 per square foot, ceramic is $6.50 for a quality tile and subfloor, and carpet comes in at $4.25 including pad and installation. These numbers are subject to constant change and I update them after every project. With this comprehensive spreadsheet in hand, I have a baseline plan that is easy to revise when changes occur and updates are warranted.

Even when you have a plan in place, it won't get you very far unless you follow through to make sure it happens. You'll see what I mean in this story:

> *A customer wanted us to remove a wall between the kitchen and family room of a large home. This wasn't difficult because the wall was not structural, although it was riddled with TV wires and switches that would need to be relocated.*

> *After discussing a plan with the contracting team, we decided to build two new columns to house the wiring and switches. These new columns would accompany one existing structural post at the side of the room. When the demo was completed, the team sent pictures that confirmed things were progressing as planned; everything was clean and organized.*

> *The contractor explained that two posts had been added in the center of the*

opening to house the new wiring, and they would be finished to match the existing corner bearing post. But there was a problem. Because of the quick turnaround, he couldn't find the same type of wood product used on the existing fluted columns in the room. Knowing that mismatched columns would be a disaster, we scrapped that plan and decided to eliminate the two columns and relocate all the wiring inside the existing bearing post. We would then balance the post and 2-foot wall with the similar configuration on the other side. This solution would address the wiring and switches while keeping the center area completely open. We agreed that our strategy was a no-brainer because it would be best for everyone involved, especially the customer.

The next morning, I received a photo that nearly knocked me out of my chair. The image depicted a wall that was completely closed in, except for a 5-foot opening that looked like a doorway into the kitchen. How does something like this happen? We had removed a full wall only to add a full wall back in. And, of course, we would be removing it again.

It's hard to achieve success in this business unless you have a solid team that communicates effectively. Everything on a rehab site is fluid and that means everything is open to interpretation. Even when you have the best intentions, things can go sideways. Make sure everyone is on the same page.

> **Mark-It**: Hire people who share your vision. Then check in often and use photographs to confirm that your projects are progressing as planned.

Support your team. Your general contractor (GC) may be your most critical hire because the two of you need to be in lock step. You will be working together to navigate daily twists and turns. Functioning like a construction manager, your GC will hire and manage the on-site work team, provide cost estimates, and develop the scope of work for each phase of the project such as plumbing and electrical rough-ins, final inspections, and more. The GC may also provide a technical skill—such as carpentry or painting—to fulfill some of your key project needs. You'll soon learn why smart team players like Shawn, my general contractor, are hard to find and valuable to keep.

Make sure your GC understands that you expect good estimates up front and plan to live as close to those projections as possible. While you need to understand all of your project's phases, costs, and details, you will issue one check to the general contractor who will then compensate the subcontractors. However, as your experience develops, you may prefer to hire your own subcontractors for key phases. For example, I use the same kitchen designer and landscaper on every project because their talents are invaluable to the success of my brand.

> **Mark-It**: **If you decide to hire your own subcontractors, be prepared to invest extra management time and effort since this will not fall under the scope of your GC. Even if your GC is willing to help, the communication will be awkward with too many people calling the shots. Nobody likes having two bosses. Shoot, most people don't like having one boss. You get my drift.**

Learn the quirks. Contractors have unique characteristics and I've learned to spot them. You'll find some generalizations here, so take this with a grain of salt. First, painters tend to be the neediest. They are hard to find, often don't show up, and like to be paid every ten minutes. Electricians are fine with being paid at the end of the job while plumbers expect an upfront draw with the remainder at the end. These might seem like unimportant tiny details, but with multiple workers on a variety of sites, the silliest minutiae can turn into a mountain of time-consuming nonsense.

Manage the complexities. To make things more interesting, some projects may have sub-subcontractors. For example, a GC might hire a roofer who also has a siding company. In this case, the GC will pay the roofer who then subcontracts the siding work, creating three layers of communication challenges. As you can imagine, one job site can become a zoo of people wanting direction, answers, and money.

> **Mark-It**: **The more moving parts you have, the more complicated your project will become. It's your job to understand the pieces and avoid the layers.**

Managing and running several projects can be daunting. It's not a hobby. It's a business, with real people whose livelihoods depend in part on you.

Know your place. Once you've assembled the team, focus on what *you* bring to the table and put your talents to their best use. Some people are managers, CEOs, or skilled workers while others prefer to come and go as they please. Wherever you fall in that range, if you are not the CEO or management type, then running a rehab business is probably not for you. Being a skilled carpenter or an experienced electrician is great. You can make a lot of money as a contractor but getting into rehabbing multiple homes as a business may not be your forte. Recognize your capabilities early on and understand the value of a business model that includes a CEO, a GC, contractors, subcontractors and sub-subcontractors.

> <u>Mark-It</u>: **As the company owner, it's not your job to run wiring, hammer nails, and do demolitions.**

It's all fun and games when people watch TV's *Property Brothers* beat down drywall on demo day but that's not where you want to be on a regular basis. While it creates a nice TV episode, in real life that type of involvement can actually be a detriment.

Throughout my life, I've amassed morsels of knowledge and tidbits of experience in carpentry, HVAC, plumbing, electrical systems, and more. While that knowledge provides a solid foundation, I now rely on people who are much more talented than I am to handle those responsibilities. Remember, I learned most of what I know about electricity as a child tinkering with wires under a model train table. I am not an expert electrician or a master plumber or an HVAC tech. I leave that work to the pros.

As your workload increases, you will appreciate the value of defining your role and building a team. Through years of managing projects for department stores, I led teams of supervisors, designers, and laborers. After venturing out on my own, I realized that I could have done so much more to help these workers achieve their full potential. Today, I focus on managing projects, removing obstacles, and getting out of the way so skilled professionals and tradespeople can do their best work.

By fulfilling my role and building a trusted team, I am freed to lead. That means I have agents finding properties, general contractors managing schedules, and bookkeepers tracking progress. One of the best ways to find these talented team members is through word of mouth. Aligning with good people and trusting them to do their jobs allows me to be nimble and work on what I do best and enjoy most: finding and designing the next project.

> **Mark-It**: Once the team is assembled, your ability to delegate both responsibility and accountability requires a willingness to relinquish a portion of your most valuable assets: money and control. Build this into your business model. Provide clear direction, re-evaluate progress on a regular basis, and be open to change.

A simple change can have a big impact. A few years ago, I realized I couldn't keep up with the constant phone calls, planning, follow up, and surprises that came at me every day. I needed to let go and let someone else help. I now have an administrator, Donna, who handles these responsibilities better than I could dream of doing. She stays ahead of meetings, emails, invoices, and more. Not only does Donna handle details and manage schedules, she offers creative ideas and recommends new ways to save money.

> **Mark-It**: Hire team players, communicate, let go—and watch your business grow.

Here's the bottom line. When it comes to leading a team, if you're greedy and try to save all the profit for yourself, you will end up miserable. If you insist on doing everyone else's job, you'll eat up all your time paying bills, sending out tax forms, and dealing with accounting issues. Not only will you set yourself up for disaster, you'll miss out on the parts of the business that excite you the most. Soon, you will be right back where you were for the past thirty years: feeling overwhelmed, underpaid, and uninspired. Many people in the construction world have fallen into this trap. Wired to manage everything themselves and make as much money as possible, they become overstressed and ultimately fail. It doesn't have to be that way. If you're in this business, it must mean that you love some aspect of it and hopefully it goes beyond money. Otherwise, you'll be sadly disappointed.

Today, my role is crystal clear. First and foremost, I am the visionary, the chief designer, the project manager. I am the most skilled at looking at a property, seeing the potential, putting it on paper, creating the scope, choosing the materials and colors, and overseeing the project to the end. That's where I fit in the best.

> **Mark-It: If you are starting and running a company, stay true to your own talent. This is easier said than done. It takes honest soul searching and dedication to stay on course.**

Right now I'm planning my Christmas party, as I do every year. In addition to family and friends, my guest list will include investors, real estate agents, hourly workers, contractors, subcontractors, sub-subcontractors, and suppliers. Even though my payroll says I have zero employees, it takes a team of over 70 people to make this company run. On a daily basis, I need to know what they're doing, understand their work quality, and determine how to pay them. It's easy to lose track of how many people I communicate with, negotiate with, and interact with. In fact, I didn't realize how extensive this group was until I put their names on a list. This might be the second-best reason for hosting a Christmas party.

CHAPTER 10

Taking Care of Business:
Licenses, Insurance & Other Scary Stuff

Understanding the value of insurance and licensing is another key to the long-term value of your brand. Proper coverage can be the difference between having a livelihood and losing it. Set your business up for success.

Licenses are essential in this business. First and foremost, make sure your contractors and other on-site professionals carry proper licenses and insurance for the jurisdiction where you are doing business. This is non-negotiable.

> **Mark-It:** Hiring unlicensed contractors is a recipe for disaster no matter how you slice it. Joe the Unlicensed Handyman who doesn't know what he is doing will get you in trouble. Period. The end.

Specialty trades such as carpenters and roofers may hold general licenses that fall under state regulations such as the Maryland Home Improvement Commission (MHIC), while plumbers, electricians, and others will have additional certifications such as apprentice or master.

Since I am not the one who physically does the work, I believe it would be inappropriate for me to own the MHIC license and its associated liability.

It is important to keep roles and responsibilities in mind as you develop your business strategy and make ongoing decisions. My expertise is in design and management, so I leave the structural, mechanical, electrical, plumbing, and other construction processes to the qualified tradesmen. I'll illustrate my reasoning with an example. As an owner without an MHIC license, let's say I start hammering on site and hit something mechanical or create a plumbing issue. In this case, it would be difficult to file an insurance claim to correct the construction problem since the damage was created by an unlicensed entity. This issue may be exacerbated after the house is sold if the new buyer uncovers a problem that occurred from unlicensed work. Instead, when proper credentials are in place, the buyer can resolve the issue through the insurance company of the licensee who completed the work.

Make it easy on everyone by requiring each professional on your construction team to document their insurance and licensing credentials *before* work commences. Without this, you could lose everything, even with a valid LLC in place. While the LLC will separate your personal assets from your business liabilities, there is nothing to protect you from a civil suit if an unlicensed problem arises, especially if injuries are involved.

Please, for the love of God, make sure you're properly insured. Even when all your contractors are insured, if a worker gets hurt or burns down one of your properties, you'll be in plenty of trouble unless you have insurance. Don't unnecessarily subject yourself to a devastating claim. Get a policy that covers your liability for mistakes, injuries, and other surprises. An insurance professional will guide you through the process and help you maintain the proper coverage as regulations fluctuate over time.

While we're on the subject of insurance, be sure to secure a policy on every property you buy. In fact, if you're working with lenders or banks that don't require insurance, they don't deserve your business. You need proper insurance for each property in case something happens on site. Once you own it, you are invested until the end.

To illustrate this point, let's go back to our earlier example of Rob the Rehabber who purchased a property for $100,000 and spent $50,000 to restore it in hopes of selling it for $200,000. Rob won't get a penny until he spends the $50,000 and goes to closing. Let's say Rob finishes the rehab, turns on the electric, and the property burns down due to a short in the rusted electrical box. If Rob's insurance was established on the purchase price of $100,000, the lender will get that full amount along with the property. Rob will get a big fat zero. He will lose the money he invested in the project, along with any profit he had hoped to make.

Don't cut corners. Get the right insurance for your projects to cover your investment. There are specific policies to protect you from all types of situations; make it a priority to talk to an insurance specialist who can explain your options. Typically, companies will offer a vacant house insurance policy—which is more expensive—that covers the property while it is empty and susceptible to vandalism. In addition, there are construction policies that cover projects in process, including the contractors working on site.

I'll sum it up this way. When you drop your phone in the toilet—everyone has done that, right?—it might seem like a big deal, but it's actually very easy to replace. Running a company is the exact opposite. Managing big projects carries a lot of risk, and when things go down the tank, it may be almost impossible to recover. Protect your company from a fall.

CHAPTER 11

Facing the Music:
Death, Taxes, Accountants & Attorneys

If you're like me, you gravitated to this business because of things you know and love, but you'll still encounter some unpleasantries along the way. Although they can't be avoided, if you know how to handle these things, they might turn out to be alright after all.

First up, death. Okay, this subject is definitely not pleasant, but don't panic. It doesn't mean this business is going to kill you—although it could. After all, it's complicated. If you've ever seen a stack of settlement papers, you know what I mean. There are folders filled with addenda and disclosures and all sorts of things that are there to protect you, the buyer, the government, and everyone in between. Being a rehabber adds complexity because you're not just purchasing one dream home; you'll be buying multiple properties on a regular basis. It's your job to understand the paperwork without drowning in it.

Speaking of death, have you thought about who would run your business if something happens to you? Whether you're 23 or 50-something like I am, there are no guarantees. Anyone could go at any time. Even if the company you are running is small, your responsibilities are substantial. You manage multiple pieces of real estate, are on the hook for a variety of loans, and have people depending on you. You owe money for labor, materials, taxes, and more. Don't dump all that on your family unless they have the skills and information to handle it.

> **Mark-It**: **Designate the person who will be capable of selling the real estate, liquidating the assets, and ensuring that all outstanding work is completed if you're not around to help.**

The sad truth is that there could be millions of dollars at risk, and if the executor doesn't understand how the business works, the system could crash and leave your loved ones with a mess. As your business evolves, avoid this type of disaster by having regular talks with your executor to clearly define responsibilities and account access.

Of course this section isn't really about dying; it's about the potential to create a mess in this business. Most days, I'd just like to focus on getting through my morning walk and finishing this book, but it's never that simple. Without the right planning, any of us could end up with financial turmoil, title problems, deed issues, and more. The list is endless, and we encounter new obstacles every day.

Make tax time easier. As if death isn't scary enough, you'll also encounter terrifying tax stuff along the way. In this business, you'll constantly be dealing with large sums of cash, so taxes can take you down quickly if you don't know what you're doing. This next statement should go without saying, but I'll mention it anyway. Make sure everything you do is above board. There are enough pitfalls in this business without coloring outside the lines and inviting the IRS to hop on your back. Even if you think you are doing things right but accidentally miss something important, the IRS could take your business. And they don't necessarily care about your personal assets and limited liability. They just want their money.

I'm not an expert in tax law but I can attest to the importance of surrounding yourself with professionals who are. Like contractors, it's hard to find a financial advisor who understands you, but when you do, the difference is huge. Not only will your daily expenses be accurately tracked, but your financial matters will be updated and documented throughout the year, making tax time a breeze. Okay, tax time is never a breeze, but the winds are more likely to be in your favor when you hire an accountant who understands LLCs.

> **Mark-It**: **If necessary, your accountant can help you set up a tax payment plan with the government at interest rates that are often far better than using your own hard money lender. These notes are typically paid off as an added amount in your taxes over time.**

Regardless of your company's size, get a good accountant to help you manage the process. You'll soon find that—contrary to popular belief—the tax man is actually easy to work with. Here's a typical scenario.

> *It's year end and you're reflecting on the past 12 months, during which you built beautiful projects that outperformed plan. You also know there were some deals that failed miserably with problems like septic system replacements and unplanned roof repairs. After the final calculations, it's clear that you barely broke even and sometimes lost money along the way. Because you're busy running the business and trying to keep up with these records in the wee hours of the morning, you might miss opportunities and become more vulnerable to ridiculous year-end tax surprises that could ruin you. Thankfully, your accountant can work magic to mitigate losses and use the gains to your benefit from a tax perspective.*

In addition to benefitting from helpful people, your business depends on solid processes. Utilize a robust financial platform such as QuickBooks to manage your accounts, pay contractors, and report earnings. These programs make it easy to set up contractors and facilitate the invoicing process.

> **Mark-It**: **I gained time and efficiency by transferring several account management functions to my administrator, who streamlines daily business transactions and minimizes challenges at tax time.**

There is a lot of bartering in this business. You'll develop relationships with an endless list of people who build, service, and provide materials for houses. In fact, I'm guessing you probably live in a house, maybe with a family, and, possibly, a dog. Naturally, some of the goods and services you encounter at work could come in handy at your house. There is nothing wrong with following through on this as long as you inform your accountant and document things properly. Be honest with your accountant, explain what you want to accomplish, and address issues through the proper channels. It's okay to have your landscaper conduct weekly maintenance at your personal residence; just be sure to account for it correctly. If you buy extra appliances and want to trade a refrigerator for some painting work in your kitchen and family room, this is fine. Let your accountant know so it can be reflected in the books.

> **Mark-It**: **Don't keep secrets from the people who help you run the business. They are there to help you succeed. You may not always like what they have to say, but I can assure you that, when it comes to financial matters, they are better at knowing the right answers than you are. Listen to them.**

Lawyers get a bad rap but you really do need them. If you're still reading this chapter, you must be serious about this business. Good for you. Now let's talk about attorneys. Finding a good one is difficult. Here's the deal: you don't need a criminal law specialist helping you with your land title issue. Look for an attorney that excels in real estate law. Get the right person with the right specialty in the right role.

When it comes to real estate settlements, title attorneys are the most efficient and cost-effective. You'll pay them a flat fee at closing. Beyond these law professionals, there are never-ending reasons to have a business attorney on retainer. Expect to pay a monthly fee for things such as lender contracts, legal battles over covenants and restrictions, lot subdivisions, title issues, claims, mechanics liens from properties bought at auction, and more. Basically, I pay my attorney to keep things from biting me. Once you develop a relationship with an attorney who immediately returns your calls and follows up without fail, you'll stop being leery of lawyers and build trust.

> **Mark-It:** **I've learned that side conversations with my attorney are invaluable, and he is often the one who sends up a warning flag when I can't see the forest for the trees.**

He has the guts to remind me that there will always be another house or property out there without a red flag.

I've addressed a lot of scary subjects head on to help you in the long run. If you get into this business without preparing for the inevitable—such as death, taxes, accountants, and attorneys—then you'll miss out on incredible possibilities. Get a team of professionals on your side and stay ahead of the game. Face the unavoidable truths and overcome the scary stuff. You'll be better for it.

CHAPTER 12

Buying & Selling:
Real Estate Brokers & Agents

Although I never became a Realtor, getting a real estate license was one of the best things I ever did. Contrary to popular belief, a real estate license isn't easy to come by or to keep. In addition to enduring hours of studying and test-taking, licensed agents are required to enroll in continuing education programs to stay current on codes and procedures. While I never intended to make a career of real estate, getting a license gave me an opportunity to see different styles of houses, observe derelict conditions in existing structures, and understand the market. Most of all, I gained an appreciation for agents and what they bring to the table: explaining processes, interpreting ever-changing laws, and connecting people. Without these professionals, I wouldn't be where I am today.

By nature, the rehabbing industry is closely linked to the real estate world. Whether you're involved with land, rental properties, or houses for sale, it all comes down to real estate. Finding worthwhile properties is easier when you surround yourself with people who can help you make things happen.

Mark-It: Agents are a key part of my team, providing me with early access to investors and resellers. They know how to determine the viability of deals, navigate paperwork, understand hidden costs, calculate value, and mitigate unnecessary risks. That's not my forte so I'm glad it's theirs.

Partner with a broker you can trust. As you evaluate brokers for a potential partnership, ask these questions: Are they part of the local community? Do they communicate easily with public works and other jurisdictions? Do they own real estate in the area? Is their office local? What is the scope of their political, social, and business network? How do they give back to the community and invest in hometown issues?

I chose Garceau Realty for several reasons. First and foremost, Georgeanna Garceau is part of the local community and she understands the surrounding market. As a small boutique firm with a strong network, Garceau specializes in Harford County and the northern Baltimore region. This access to a connected local spectrum has been pivotal for my business.

One agent, Dale, handles my transactions from the front-end sale all the way through to closing. Over the years, this valuable partnership has been a mecca for connecting me with clients who want to modify plans or rescue older homes. These referral experiences helped me realize that many people who are interested in homes with timeless character ultimately walk away from their dream for one reason or another. Afraid that they don't have the time, money, or expertise to take on the project, these visionaries settle for something much less than they truly want, with inferior construction and design. Dale helps us all navigate the process.

When you help each other, everyone wins. Working with Dale, I typically manage seven to ten projects per year, many of which are distressed properties that provide a front-end buyer broker commission of 2% or less. On the back end, the newly-renovated property is typically sold at the top of the market with a full broker commission. So, although my agent's front-end opportunity on these deals is minimal, he benefits on both ends of the transaction. With ten deals per year, I am basically delivering 20 payable transactions.

But that's only the start. Over time, all the listings, advertising, and open houses produce spinoffs. It's not unusual for people to come in for one open house, learn about another listing, and follow up with a purchase. The best offshoot opportunities happen when the original house sells before the open house even starts. Dale facilitates the process by helping buyers list their existing homes so they can move forward more quickly. If my rehab doesn't work for them, Dale guides them to one that does. It's easy to see how partnering with an agent is a win-win scenario. While Dale brings me buyers and expedites the process, I help him transform 20-plus yearly transactions into 30 or more. As a result, the volume of business I create for the broker often exceeds that of a majority of licensed real estate agents.

> **<u>Mark-It</u>: By sharing the workload and contributing to the broker's overall success, you will earn access to valuable benefits.**

In addition to the property sale and settlement benefits, there are a host of reasons to connect with a real estate broker and establish an ongoing agent relationship. Even though I'm not an active real estate agent, Garceau provides me with an office in their building, where I can meet clients and conduct business. I'm considered part of the team when it comes to resources, networking, and inclusion in parties and events. No doubt, some of the people who work there don't even realize that I'm not an actual agent. We work together and share ideas, especially when it comes to buying and selling distressed properties.

A good broker will help you build credibility and strengthen your brand. Being part of this broker/agent world has immeasurably legitimized my work and positively impacted my success in the rehab business. My brand is strengthened when my company name and projects are linked to Garceau's in ads, signs, and promotions. In our market, customers already know and respect the Garceau name, providing me with credibility through association. This type of trusted relationship goes a long way in setting me apart from everyday flippers.

Some people in this business don't see the value of working with agents. On the contrary, I wouldn't do a project without a real estate agent. These professionals are my competitive advantage, a valuable link to people I wouldn't otherwise meet. With Garceau's involvement,

I minimize the competition and negotiate better pricing. Their agents recommend me to customers in need of a rehabber and provide the inside scoop on upcoming properties. I take every opportunity to get my work in front of them: going to open houses, sitting through lunches, and participating in bar fests.

> **Mark-It: Real estate agents fuel my business and keep things from coming at me by surprise.**

Garceau Realty and RR Projects & Design are companies run by people who care. If something goes astray, I have Georgeanna's back and she has mine. Like my relationship with Dale, we advise each other on listings, industry updates, and more. I cannot overemphasize the value this partnership.

If you skimmed through this chapter, here's what you need to know. Find a good broker. Build trust. Help each other. Enjoy the benefits.

CHAPTER 13

Get Your Head Examined

If you're planning to get into the rehab business or buy a rescued home, I've laid out many things to know before you look at a property or write the first check. These basic but important issues include: strategies, money, contractors, insurance, liabilities, brokers, and more. By now, I hope you're getting a feel for the amount of risk and reward that accompanies the rehab world.

As an up-and-coming rehabber, if you don't know what you're dealing with, you could be headed for trouble and might want to question your sanity. Likewise, buyers of rescued properties should approach the process with eyes open. Be on the lookout for flippers who turn out work that doesn't fit your parameters.

> **Mark-It: Regardless of where you are in the rehab spectrum, when something doesn't add up, ask questions and be willing to move on to another project that does.**

If you plan to become a business owner, understand that you will be impacting lives. A lot of them. For starters, there's you and your family, followed by people who work for you, their families, and all the folks that will one day live in the homes you touch. You can't go into this business on a whim. With this in mind, my advice is to get your head examined *before* you jump in. How do you do that? Start by having a down-to-earth conversation with yourself.

> **<u>Mark-It</u>: Look in the mirror and determine if you have the mental stamina and financial fortitude to follow your dream.**

Once you've convinced yourself that you're ready to get into the rehab business, don't stop there. Do some research. Talk to people around you and listen intently when your friends in their standard 9 to 5 jobs tell you that you're crazy. Read books, attend lectures, and arm yourself with the information you need to move forward with your eyes open. Then get to the heart of the matter. Talk to a competent professional—an effective sounding board who understands that risk in life is part of the reward. Believe it or not, this same process applies to buyers of rehabbed properties. Do your homework, define your commitment, understand your risks, and make sure your rehabber's dedication and vision match yours.

After all the research and soul-searching, if you're still onboard with your passion for the rehab business, be inspired by the fact that people just like you have managed to make the transition. I was once exactly where you are, wondering if I had the guts to get something more out of life.

You're almost there. Wrap your head around what you're doing, understand the risk, take a dose of reality—and get ready to enjoy the ride.

PART THREE

THE SEARCH

In my leap of faith, the only thing I would have changed was to jump sooner.

CHAPTER 14

Going Once ...
Tax Sales & Auctions

Now that you're on your way, this section will provide insights to guide your decisions. With experience, you'll recognize warning signs and exploit the right deals when they come along.

There are endless ways to find new projects, as you'll soon learn. Before I get into that, let's talk about site visits. These road trips allow you to compare an eager seller's dressed-up property description with the actual house standing bare in its birthday suit. On such visits, I often look at properties that don't turn into projects until a year later. And, oh God, I've found some things ... like this house:

> It was a big, beautiful rural estate on multiple acres of land with a horse farm, stables, and a pool. The house was gorgeous, but sadly the whole place had fallen into disrepair. A wealthy couple owned the house from the beginning, lingering there after raising three daughters who had long since moved away. At least that's how I think the story went when I pieced it together from remnants left in the house ... belongings that stayed put when the humans departed.

Upon visiting the property, I characterized the original owners as a well-to-do, big-company executive and his wife. No doubt, they loved the house and lived there until one of them became ill or passed away and the other one ultimately moved out. It was obvious that they had reached the stage of life that required outfitting a main-level bedroom with medical equipment. I can always tell when that has happened.

What I couldn't understand was how the house had fallen into such disrepair. Who knew the time and cost impact of myriad issues the inhabitants endured? I surmised that they had amassed a mountain of expenses related to dealing with the property and attending to a variety of health problems.

In situations like this, a reverse mortgage is often a contributing culprit. Of course, there's nothing wrong with reverse mortgages; they serve a purpose if you're not planning to leave millions of dollars to your estate. Quite honestly, if you bought a house, put money into it and maintained it as you grew old, why shouldn't you reap the benefits of everything you invested? As long as it's not a predatory loan, but a true, clean reverse mortgage— reviewed by an attorney to ensure that it aligns with your timing needs without jeopardizing your living arrangements—you are good to go.

From my vantage point, it appeared that the reverse mortgage had been created after the wife had passed and the husband's health began failing. Regardless of the reason, the husband and a few personal belongings had been moved out of a spectacular house that sat and waited like a loyal puppy while the reverse mortgage payments gave it no attention at all.

I later learned that my suppositions were fairly accurate. Unaware of the exact details surrounding the reverse mortgage, the extended family was left to deal with: a) the health and well-being of the father, and b) the fact that the entire estate was losing property value and slowly dwindling away. In the end, the reverse mortgage sucked all the equity out of the estate, leaving the bank with no choice but to foreclose. This is a textbook example of how a reverse mortgage can drain the life out of a beautiful home owned by wealthy people with good intentions.

By the time we first set foot on the property it was in a state of suspended animation, having succumbed to more than five years of neglect. As you can imagine, the scene was ugly. Pipes had burst in an upstairs bathroom sending water and debris into the main level kitchen before collapsing to the basement. The contrast of this devastating destruction in such a gracious residence is hard to describe. In one direction, I saw mold, drywall, dirt, and mess. Another glance revealed a family room filled with high-end collectibles, fashionable furniture, and magazines on the coffee table.

Artifacts of life—they pull me in and won't let go. For me, this is the hard part: seeing just enough of what used to be. I envisioned a family gathered around the kitchen hearth. Although dated, the appliances were high end, the dishwasher was signaling that the contents inside were clean, and the pantry was still stocked with food. The house looked ready for its inhabitants to start their evening dinner routine; yet, things were severely amiss. Someone had leaned a board across the back door to prevent access even with a key. The house had become a wildlife preserve, with birds and rodents entering through the chimney and broken windows.

Other than the kitchen, the main floor was somewhat stable except for portions of the family room that showed the rigors of time and water damage. In the study, stacks of guns and wall-hung taxidermy told the story of a hunter and gun collector. With evidence of black mold and moisture eating into natural materials here and there, I knew the house was at risk of structural damage.

The second floor was relatively intact, as if the family had been forced to leave on a moment's notice. There were clothes in the closets, medicines in the bathroom, and books on side tables. Thankfully, the roof was not leaking, but the rooms were full of stink bugs and I discovered the remnants of a small cat. Sadly, it's hard to say how long the poor creature had survived.

Many devastating consequences of long-term neglect were in the basement, thanks to gravity's persistent work. In the lowest level of the house, everything was damp and covered in mold. Wearing masks and carrying flashlights, we took in the soggy, black-coated view: taxidermy, gym equipment, a sauna, Christmas decorations, furniture, a workshop, a toppled safe, and more guns. And then, evidence of an intruder via a broken basement access door that channeled seepage from overflowing rear porch gutters. Who knew how long water had been sneaking behind the electrical panels and causing wires to rust? I made a mental note that the electrical system would need to be removed and reinstalled.

Outside, the house was surrounded by magnificent features, including a spacious pool, still holding water. Four walkways converged at a garden with a gazebo and trellises framed by white fencing. The patio furniture was still in place, with metal frames and thick, green cushions that were split and spilling ample stuffing for a forest of birds' nests. While most of the awnings were retracted, one had blown off, and water leaks were eating into an exterior porch structure that looked repairable. Overgrown, unruly, and surreal, I could imagine the scene's glorious past.

As I walked the site, the only visible sign of care was in the stable, where three horses had been left in the capable hands of a neighbor. Located far from the house, this attentiveness had little impact on the overall estate. The home's detached garage held three vehicles standing in wait: an old model Cadillac, a pickup truck, and a smaller car. Above the garage was an office cooled by air conditioning from power that was functioning on the summer day I visited. Sealed up tight, this upper-level office had been preserved much better than the house itself. Papers on the desk and taxidermy on the walls hinted that it might have been the husband's office.

In this upstairs space, I noticed that a refrigerator was still running. This reminds me of an important point you need to know about every distressed property you visit. NEVER, EVER open the refrigerator—unless you are looking for trouble. Don't ask questions. Put a rope around it and have your contractor wheel it to the dumpster. Do not—under any circumstances—open the door. After years of neglect, old houses develop a dark sense of humor and old refrigerators are just one way of expressing it.

In the end, I decided to make an offer on the property. Unfortunately, the estate underwent a major legal dispute that prompted the bank to foreclose on the property, launching a typical scenario. The house would sit and wait for over six months until the bank assigned someone to market a property he knew nothing about. Banks don't always understand a home's worth or the value of its artifacts. In cases like this, the person assigned to clean the house might end up selling relics for thousands of dollars in profit that the bank will never know about. An overpriced house will be placed on the market, enduring more time and nonsense until it finds its way back down to the original offer. It's a sad situation that happens far too often.

The rehab business is about timing. While handling three other projects, I didn't have the wherewithal or the funding to wait for months while this process played out. This house ended up in the hands of a buyer who wanted to restore it and live there. Although that made me feel better, I had a vision for the house, and it hurt to let go.

You might call it paradise lost.

The people who originally lived in that home—like so many others I have visited—must have collected for a lifetime, gathering trunkloads of memories that were eventually covered in layers of mold and dirt. It's a killer—it truly is a killer—to watch this. My imagination runs wild trying to fill in the blanks of stories I can't quite understand. When I rescue a house, it is my job to uncover the history, assemble broken pieces of the past, and find a starting point to rebuild it.

After touring countless properties from top to bottom, inside and out, I realize this is where my skills come in. Deep down, I know I'm good at this. I can look at—and through, and past—a home's current situation without clouding my view of its potential. It's not just about the structure and the work to be done. I've learned how to look at it all, envision the possibilities, add up the costs, and determine the price someone will pay me to breathe the life back in.

First, I have to find the right properties. A common and cost-effective source is the live auction, and there are several types.

Live Auction #1: Tax Sales on the Courthouse Steps

Most people are familiar with county or state auctions conducted on the courthouse steps. Also known as tax sales, these auctions involve properties that are being sold due to nonpayment of assessments. Here's how they work. If an owner fails to pay taxes for a few years, the government may seize the property, hoping it can be sold to someone who will cover the overdue expenses and ultimately take possession.

It's likely that a person who is underwater on taxes hasn't kept up with mortgage payments either, so the bank may seek to protect its lienholder interest by covering the taxes to keep it off the auction block. If there is little or no outstanding mortgage to be recouped by the lender, the bank's interest is devalued and the property may be released to auction. In these cases, a bank representative will attend the auction and determine the best course of action. Often, the price begins at the full amount of taxes owed and decreases from there. Occasionally, the bank will buy back its own property at a lower rate. This is risky because another bidder could take ownership of the property at a discounted amount that is still higher than what the bank wants to pay. Since this situation may make a property seem more attractive, it pays to learn the back story before you fall in love with it.

When a property reaches the auction stage, both an owner and the bank have likely determined that the taxes owed will cost more than it is worth. This means you have found something that is already questionable in value.

> **Mark-It**: **By the time a property gets to the courthouse steps, odds are not in your favor that you will steal a rockstar property at a rock-bottom price.**

Understanding how properties come to the courthouse steps is every bit as important as knowing what to do at the auction. Your established partnerships with real estate agents and attorneys will help you navigate the details. Tread carefully.

Research everything—before you buy. Go into auctions with your eyes open. With a lot of knowledge and a little luck, now and then you'll discover a rare, fantastic deal that makes it to auction. Perhaps an estranged parent passed away with no will in place, sending a valuable estate into the government's hands. With the property dropped in their laps, local officials often send it to auction knowing that any money acquired is better than none. Voila! You may have found a gold mine.

To identify these gems, you need to know everything you can about a property before you arrive at the courthouse steps. Start by looking online or in your local newspaper. State and county regulations require properties eligible for auction to be posted in print and on the Internet for a specific time period to ensure that all interested parties are notified. "Interested parties" doesn't refer to people who might be interested in the property; they are heirs or stakeholders who have related financial or legal rights.

Dig deeper. At this point, in terms of research, you've only scratched the surface. When the deed transfers title at auction, the bank will lose ownership interest in the property and be left with an outstanding note that has nothing to do with the new buyer, limiting its ability to collect unresolved tax liens. While you should be able to purchase the property clear of these encumbrances, you may be liable for mechanics liens associated with unpaid contracting work. For example, if a contractor has a mechanics lien on the property for $20,000 when the back taxes stand at $10,000, he has the right to exercise an ownership stake in the property and take possession of it prior to auction. These types of liens tend to run with the property, allowing contractors to file suits to collect outstanding funds even against a new owner. It's rare, but it happens. Do your research.

Watch for changes. Once the notifications have been issued, the auction date will be assigned. If the current owners have encountered difficult financial times and want to retain it, they can reset the clock and hold the property with a single payment. Remember, government entities do not want the property back, so they can work with the owners, agree on an amount, and start the whole process over again. While this doesn't mean the debt has been repaid, the property owners have the opportunity to negotiate and retain the property right up to the auction date. The cumulative result of these situations is that often more than half the properties listed on tax sale sites will be unavailable by the day of the auction.

Know your limit—and stick with it. After fully researching the property, you'll determine how much you are willing to pay for it— before you arrive at the courthouse steps. In most cases, you will not have the opportunity to tour the house and assess its condition other than a drive-by observation. Because of this, I recommend assuming a worst-case scenario.

> **Mark-It: You should plan to buy the property at no more than 50% of its perceived value compared with similar houses in the neighborhood.**

Since you know nothing about the interior of the home, you have to expect the worst. Be prepared to stay at or below the maximum amount you are willing to pay and stand your ground. Trust me, it isn't easy and I have seen many people get sucked into the frenzy of an auction. If you're a gambler, love Vegas, and are addicted to winning at any cost, auctions are not a good place for you. On the other hand, if you approach Vegas like I do, you'll be fine. When I go to Vegas, I keep a set dollar amount in my pocket for the evening. My perspective is that I'm on vacation and willing to spend that money—let's say it's $1,000—for some nonsense fun whether it's dinner, a show, or time in the casino. No matter what, when I run out of that $1,000, I'm done for the day and I don't spend any more. If I win money that exceeds this amount, I keep my winnings, standing firm on my original commitment. By treating auctions this way, I've avoided falling into a trap of bidding up something that is not worth a higher price.

Play your cards right. A lot of people at auctions are giant losers but that doesn't have to be you. Much like Vegas, at an auction you are playing against the house. The house knows all the rules—the state or county has the inside scoop—so the auction is not geared in your favor. To increase your odds of playing against the house, start by understanding what is owed on the property you're looking at. If a house is worth $100,000 with $20,000 in back taxes, you know the county wants its $20,000, and you might have calculated a bid limit of $50,000. Although they'd be happy to make more, the county is mainly interested in collecting its $20,000, so once the bidding goes above that amount you are lining their pockets. That might be okay if you know the property is worth it, but remember, they have knowledge that you don't.

> **Mark-It: As a general rule, I do not bid much above the owed tax amount and/or a combination of that and my assessed value.**

What happens at an auction? It's pretty much like everything you've imagined from movies and TV shows. A stereotypical government official appears with a clipboard, wearing a lanyard ID badge over a tie that's too short. He announces the properties printed on the sheet, taking bids according to the exact minute noted, skipping those that are no longer available. In some cases, auctions provide only a general starting time, so you need to be prepared in case other properties drop off and yours comes up earlier than expected.

In addition to times, the auction notice will state how much cash is needed to take possession of the property and the number of days you will have to provide the remaining funds to complete the purchase. For example, if $20,000 is required up front, you need to appear at the auction with a $20,000 cashier's check—not cash. As a winning bidder, you'll turn over that amount at the auction and then sign papers stating when you will submit the remaining money. Although some auction officials will demand proof of funds, they don't care if you use a hard money lender or have cash in the bank. This evidence could be supplied in the form of a bank statement, a confirmation letter from a lender, a savings account, or similar means. I have established working relationships with multiple lenders who can provide this type of confirmation when needed. Be forewarned: if you don't have the money to pay the remaining funds for the note in the time specified, the county can retain the property along with your deposit check. That means you could lose your $20,000. No kidding.

Expect company. Of course, you are not doing this in a vacuum so you will have to deal with other bidders. The bank's representative will likely show up and may be willing to accept a discounted rate. In addition, you'll run into a variety of wholesalers who have done their research, can deliver cash, and are ready to buy. Don't be surprised by them. The most distressing fellow bidders you will encounter are the Idealists. They are a buzzkill in my business. With no idea what they are doing, these people drive up the bid amount while letting everyone else down. They are the wild card, bidding with heart, not head. Unpredictable and naive, they often overpay their way into buyer's remorse. As Idealists escalate the bids, the bank and wholesalers will drop out and you'll be left watching the train wreck. I've seen it happen and it's not pretty. Don't let them suck you into overbidding.

> <u>Mark-It</u>: **No matter how much you love the house or property being auctioned, do your homework, know your number, and stick with it.**

While fun to watch, interesting to observe, and successful for some, the courthouse step option has never really panned out for me. I won't say it never works, but be advised that it is very rare to stroll up to the courthouse steps and walk away with a deal.

Live Auction #2: Estate Sales

Another type of live auction is an estate sale organized through a professional auction house. Often advertised online and in the newspaper, these events are established to auction off property and personal belongings in the house. I like antiques, so I have to manage my time carefully at auctions. I could spend all day looking at cool stuff and never find a project.

Ask about reserves. In most cases, estate auctions come about when heirs suddenly find themselves with property to sell. While a good auction house will provide guidance, heirs often want to move quickly and this impatience creates the opportunity for bargains. The auction house will usually set a reserve so it won't be obligated to sell the property below a specified price. In rare, time-critical instances, you might find a no-reserve auction where the property simply goes to the highest bidder. Research will help you understand how the reserve fits into your business strategy.

Get the scoop on previews and deposits. Estate auctions operate a lot like tax sales; management will specify the deposit required on site along with the time period allotted to produce the remaining funds. Occasionally, you'll have the opportunity to preview the property on advertised days or on the morning of the auction. Develop your worst-case scenario and adjust it as appropriate based on observed property updates or renovations.

Define the challenges. While properties at estate sales typically pass cleanly and traditionally through a title company without fear of encumbrances, you may encounter issues similar to those at a tax sale. For one, you'll be bidding against competitors that include bona fide rehabbers like me, along with flippers who drive up the price based on the limited time and money they plan to invest in the project. Next, you'll find the worst-case scenario: Idealists come out in droves for these sales. If Idealists latch onto a property, they may be willing to pay whatever it takes to get it. More often than not, these dream-oriented buyers drive the price up and prevail in the end. When this happens, I commiserate with my counterparts in the business who would normally be competitors. Attending all the same sales, we exchange niceties and share hellos on friendly terms until the bidding starts. As soon as the

Idealists start driving up the price, these competitors become my best friends and we kibitz: "What are they doing? How will they pay for this? I heard they bought it for their parents. They'll never get over this hurdle! I don't know what they're going to do!" The one time I am in unison with my rivals is when we are up against the I-don't-know-what-I'm-doing people. In this way, the Idealists unite us.

I rarely attend auctions because, quite frankly, they can be a huge waste of time. Before you head out to an auction, let me share a story to prepare you.

The house intrigued me. It was a classic farmhouse layered with gothic Victorian details. Situated on nine acres of land, it had plenty of potential as a horse farm or subdivided property. But it needed work—a lot of work. That made me think it might be the perfect opportunity to pick up a property that was too much for a flipper but just right for me.

Before I got too excited about the house, Dale and I did our due diligence, checking out the septic and well, learning about the owners, and determining how long it had been on the market. This was a live public auction that would be held on site but we had the opportunity to pre-inspect the property, make notes, and take pictures prior to the sale. We went over it with a fine-toothed comb and liked what we found, although the kitchen had been removed, there was plastic wrapped around the porch, several windows had rotted, the interior was exposed, the baths were not functional, and there was no power in the house. At the front of the house, the authentic Victorian details were still intact, including the original stair, bannister, trim, and plank floors. The back of the house was more modern, having been renovated about 30 years ago. The end result was an interesting mix of farmhouse style with a modern layout that included a mudroom, porches, and other features that would appeal to today's buyers.

After completing my research and investing time in this auction—while swearing I wouldn't invest time in another auction—I got a $15,000 cashier's check to cover my deposit. Unlike every other retail operation on the planet that accepts electronic payments, auctions are still run like it's the 1950s, so you can't make a bid unless you bring a cashier's check.
This auction was a public event run by a professional auctioneer who worked directly with the owner with no bank involvement and no specified reserve. Posted as an absolute auction, there was no approval needed, so the

100

house could be transferred at the final auction price. In other words, the highest bidder would take it, clean and simple.

It was an unusually hot day so after dropping off my check and signing in, I asked Dale to keep the car running with the air conditioner on as I sat in the car and made phone calls. I avoid interacting with people at auctions because a) I talk a lot and tend to give up my position, and b) it frustrates me to listen to other nonsense. Dale, on the other hand, is the social butterfly who has to walk around and see what is going on.

When the auction began, I got out of car to check out the scene. It looked like every other auction, with about 25 people gathered, a decent number for old farmhouse. Without making eye contact, I took this in, spying some typical wild-card players:

- *I overheard a mother and daughter talking about buying the house and fixing it up themselves so the daughter could live there. While they were trying their best to copy the mother-daughter team on HGTV, it was obvious they had no idea what they were doing. This was a recipe for disaster.*

- *A guy with four or five kids in tow was telling someone he would buy the house as a functional home for his large family. This, too, seemed like a long shot, as I knew there were better values out there for a family home with significantly less work.*

The bid opened with the auctioneer jabbering in the lively language that excites the crowd. We've all heard it—the real, old-school auction cadence. He started outrageously high, around $400,000, which more than doubled my limit. My number was $160,000, based on a rehab estimate of $200,000 with a potential resale of just under $500,000. There were several unknowns, so I knew rehab costs could reach as high as $250,000. If I paid $160,000 and put $250,000 into the project, it would quickly add up. I would stick to my numbers without wavering.

With no one biting on the original high amount, the bidding dropped as low as $130,000 before a bidder kicked in. As the auctioneer continued his ramblings, the amount moved up and I said nothing.

Let me stop here and explain how I approach the bid process. For starters, I stand back, watch others, and read their bids. Often, I never make a sound. If the bid quickly rises above my number, I just get in the car and leave having never disclosed anything. When I do engage, I feel my way through the bidding process in a method I like to call the popcorn strategy. For me, bids are like popcorn in a pan and I wait until only a few kernels are still popping before I act. I don't want to pull the pan off the heat too early—but I also don't want to burn the popcorn. You know what I'm talking about; you pull the pan from the heat at that magic moment when you haven't heard a pop for a few seconds. I don't really care what the bid amount is until it nears my number—and then I listen for the kernel pops. Once the pops start to spread out, I wait until last possible pop ... going once ... going twice ... and the auctioneer draws his last breath. That's when I raise my hand and pop the bid up, typically a bit more than what he would have increased it to keep someone interested.

On this day, the bids were below my number when the bidding stopped. After no bid went higher, the pops stopped and I raised my hand. One person tried to outbid me and I waited for the auctioneer to reach his final breath before popping the amount up by $5,000 to my calculated number. In the moments that followed, no one said anything and the auctioneer slammed the hammer and shouted SOLD! At that point, the only requirement was to provide the seller with my information and confirm my qualifications.

In rare cases, the seller and auctioneer may decide to reopen the bidding, determining that the on-site activity did not allow them to reach the optimal amount. Given the bidding scenario at this particular auction, this seemed unlikely, so I prepared to finalize the paperwork and buy the house.

You can imagine my surprise when the auctioneer returned to say that the seller had decided not to take the offer, was no longer selling the property, and ended the auction. This was unprecedented for me. As mentioned earlier, a) I don't like auctions in the first place and b) even after doing my research and sticking with my strategy, I had wasted my time on an absolute auction that was far from absolute. In the end, 25 people had invested time in attending an event where the auction house had done everything under the sun to get the best price for a seller who didn't follow through.

This story illustrates why I don't like auctions. If this were easy, everyone would do it. The auction world can get you excited after you do everything right and win the bid, but you still may not get the property. To the best of my knowledge, that house is still sitting there with plastic wrapped around the front porch, unsold and uncared for. And that's the saddest part of the story.

Live Auction #3: Bank Sales

Although there are many other types of live auctions, the last one I'll mention is the bank sale. In addition to standard banks, this category includes Freddie Mac, Fannie Mae, or any other type of government-backed loan. When banks or government entities acquire foreclosures, they usually assign the liquidation to an in-house asset manager who may approach the process in a variety of ways. The auction is often used as a means of determining a property's value. In this case, the asset manager sets the reserve amount—usually undisclosed—high enough to observe the bids and gain insight without actually selling the property at the initial auction. As a result, the auction is nothing more than a real estate litmus test. If you have invested extensive effort in conducting research and calculating your bid approach, these sales become big time-wasters when you realize the bank had no intention of selling and was using you and other bidders to determine a price.

> **Mark-It**: I recommend limiting your involvement with bank sales. Your time is too valuable.

In summary, of the three types of live auctions I've talked about—tax sales, estate sales, and bank sales—the one I use most is the estate sale which has occasionally provided me with successful opportunities. If you are still interested in the other two live auction types, here's my advice. Follow the auction process until the property goes through multiple price adjustments, note when it fails, and track it when it is later listed with a real estate agent. I've found success there.

Online Auctions

Online auctions are virtually live, although everything is, of course, handled through the Internet. You won't find most tax sales handled online, but you will encounter bank foreclosures and other types of estate liquidations. While many of the online activities are similar to the live auction process, I believe they offer some greater benefits.

Know the platforms. Property auctions are available via a variety of online platforms such as Hubzu—which is one of my favorites—along with large commercial sites like Zillow. Government entities operate their own online sites through HUD. Locally, I access MRIS or Bright MLS, searching for listings noted with an auction reference. Unlike live sales, most online auctions are listed with a real estate agent, directing interested parties to the corresponding website. This means you will usually have the opportunity to preview the property, walk it yourself, and do your homework. I prefer finding properties through this method because I know what I'm getting into.

Develop experience. Once you register on a few auction sites, you'll learn that the more business you do, the easier it is to find success. When you become a known entity, familiarity works to your benefit.

> **Mark-It: After creating a track record that shows you've bought seven or eight properties through a platform such as Hubzu, you will be regarded as a stronger bidder compared with first-time participants, increasing your likelihood of proceeding with a transaction.**

The drawback with online auctions is that your competition is much broader. Since Internet-based auctions are open to anyone with a computer, you may find yourself involved in a national bidding competition. However, most out-of-area bidders need a local contact for market analyses and property visits, so outsiders often steer clear.

Be realistic. With online auctions, it's easy to feel like you are dealing with play money because everything is electronic. Let's say you decide on a max bid of $130,000 and just before the auction ends, the price is at $135,000. On the screen, it looks as easy as changing a 0 to a 5, so you think: "Is $5,000 going to break my whole plan on this property?" The answer is probably no, but the auction house will likely up the ante by $5,000, placing the next bid at $140,000, which is now $10,000 above your max bid strategy. Remember, you might be lucky to clear $20,000 on a project that will demand six to nine months of your time, and in an instant, you could click away half or all of your profit. Don't let an online auction suck you into overbidding or joining in a frenzy to beat your competitors. This is not gambling. It is not a slot machine. Stick with the bid you planned.

Reap the benefits. Surprisingly, Idealists don't tend to frequent online auctions. Given the popularity of online shopping, this may seem odd, but Idealists have to fall in love with a house and that's hard to do through a computer screen. Internet-based auctions require a different vision that favors professionals. These auctions filter out overbidding and narrow the playing field through stiff guidelines that may require registration deposits and per-bid premiums of $2,500 or more. Although the bid premium is applied to the purchase price, it weeds out people who are not truly committed. Like live auctions, the online versions usually require a non-refundable deposit from the winning bidder before a contract is assigned, with the remaining funds due in a specified number of days.

> <u>Mark-It</u>: **In online auctions, front-end requirements limit participation from Idealists and non-business people, keeping the prices more realistic for professional bidders.**

With relatively smooth transactions, online auctions are my second-preferred way to buy a property (after working with a real estate agent), and I have secured some of my best deals through this method. Still, significant research is required to bid correctly and avoid pitfalls.

CHAPTER 15

The Long and Short of
Foreclosures & Short Sales

Most of the inventory in the rehab market is generated through foreclosures and short sales. Despite the financial crisis over a decade ago, the market still allows people to get into properties they truly can't afford and, sadly, that eventually comes back to haunt them. In addition, there will always be those who find themselves in short sale or foreclosure situations due to changes in health, income, or other circumstances.

Foreclosures

The bulk of these properties are bought-by-the-bank scenarios, where the lender takes back the house at the amount owed plus any outstanding fees. Let's say an amount of $50,000 is still owed on a $100,000 mortgage when payments stop and the bank buys a house back. At the time of foreclosure, the required investment will be 10% to 20% above the outstanding mortgage amount as a result of interest accrued over time and servicing fees related to debt collection.

While the bank views this 10% to 20% as part of the return owed on its investment, I classify it as excess. This is really the cost of doing business. I don't feel a responsibility to reimburse the bank for its error in lending money to the wrong people. When I make mistakes or encounter losses in my business, no one writes me a check or gives me money. Banks lead prospective buyers through an underwriting ordeal with thousands of pages of requirements over weeks of time, vetting them back and forth in order to lend them money and get them to settlement. After all this, if something goes awry it's not my problem. This is a volatile industry. We all encounter risk.

Before biting on this foreclosure opportunity, I will calculate my approach knowing that banks will do everything they can to avoid losing money.

1) First, I'll determine the bank's position by assessing the amount owed on the mortgage when the foreclosure took place. Banks have thresholds on foreclosures, and I determine my optimal negotiating position by calculating backward with this in mind. In our example, the original mortgage on the house was $100,000 and the bank took it back when $50,000 was still due. As a result, I'll discount any additional nonsense fees the bank says it is owed because that $50,000 is all the bank really has to recoup before it will be in loss territory. True, the bank will not see profit without collecting fees, but it is not taking a loss if it recovers the full amount loaned to the buyer.

   I'm not a banker, so this book is based on what I've experienced and how I do business. I use a reasonable, common-sense approach. If I know that the bank needs to recover $50,000, and has been sitting on the property for two years, I will factor in costs for taxes and winterization. I usually add about 10% for these incidentals, amounting to $5,000 in our $50,000 example. To me, that means the bank needs $55,000.

2) Next, I'll calculate my investment threshold. At an estimated market value of $150,000 after rehab, let's say the bank decides to list the foreclosure with an agent or set an auction reserve at $120,000. At that price, there is no way a rehabber can make it work. Remember, it is always my goal to acquire a distressed

property for no more than half its market value. In this case, my top investment would be $75,000. By understanding that the bank only needs to recover $55,000, I know the potential impact of my $75,000 threshold. I can further strengthen my position by coming in as a cash buyer with no strings attached, no inspections needed, and the ability to settle the deal in the next 30 days. Game over.

Finding properties through the foreclosure process is extremely dependent upon positioning, timing, and luck. Each asset manager has different goals and motivations, so houses that appear to be in the same boat at the same price will produce different outcomes, depending on the bank. One asset manager will turn down a reasonable offer, sit on the house for six more months, incur carrying costs, and take a chance on finding a better deal down the line. Another manager might want to liquidate properties and get them off the books as quickly as possible. Most are trying their best to make money on money they already made money on. Yes, you read that right. It's a merry-go-round of money.

There are people out there who will create this carousel of revenue for the asset managers, but that's not me. I do my homework, understand where the bank is in the process, track the property's time on market, and calculate the variation between the numbers stated and the numbers needed. If I know the bank needs $55,000, I might end up paying $75,000, knowing that there may be additional carrying fees that were not included in my calculations. But, if an Idealist enters the picture with a full $120,000 investment, the bank's ultimate goal will be achieved. The firm will make money on money it should have lost money on—and then make even more.

Short Sales

A short sale is basically a partial foreclosure in which the seller has negotiated an agreement with the bank to reduce the remaining mortgage amount. By agreeing to short sell the property rather than take it back, the bank allows the seller to list it at a price below the amount required to pay off the loan. Once the deal is negotiated, it's no different than a foreclosure, and the bank has to accept the agreed-upon price. As a buyer making an offer on a short sale, it is more important than ever to understand what the bank is owed. The bank will not give you a good deal on a short sale and take a ridiculous loss. If $100,000 is still owed on a $150,000 mortgage, the bank isn't going to accept $75,000 unless the house is flooded or collapsing—and then you don't want it anyway.

Despite the challenges, I've found considerable success in buying properties through foreclosures and short sales that went to auction or were listed with an agent. The biggest challenge is that they take more time. If you do this for a living and can track the process and negotiate the right price on a short sale, go for it.

If you are a homebuyer looking to purchase a short sale, be prepared to live in an apartment for six months while you wait through a long, arduous paperwork process. The ordeal has improved over the past few years, but it's still grueling.

Rich Man, Poor Man

Some of the most attractive deals involve scenarios I call "Rich Man, Poor Man" and I often find them through my agent. These are properties that become available when the mortgage is no longer affordable after a long-time owner lost a job or navigated a divorce. While these properties typically are not distressed, the owners are trying to sell them quickly to avoid foreclosure. Often, the owners can afford to sell below market value because they have already put enough upfront money into the house to keep the mortgage from being ridiculous.

While these situations usually do not lend themselves to 50%-below-market-value purchases, they often come in at around 30%. They are what I call cosmetic rehabs where, for example, the kitchen has been updated but still needs a touch of granite, paint, or refinishing. The limited renovation required allows me to push the budget a bit closer to market value—but still not above 30%.

Mom and Dad Are Gone

A similar scenario is one I've named "Mom and Dad are Gone." In this case, the original owners passed away and left the house to their kids who are hesitant to sell. As a result, the house may sit vacant for years because the children have a sentimental attachment to the place where they grew up. Even though no one lives there, the heirs try to care for the house at a distance, until it sadly deteriorates and becomes too much to manage. Typically, there is little or no mortgage remaining and by the time the family decides to sell, they want to unload it quickly. For example, if they know the home's value is $500,000 and the mortgage has been paid, it's not far-fetched to see them sell it at $250,000 or $275,000, especially if they find a cash buyer who settles quickly.

This also happens when one parent survives the other and needs proceeds from the house to cover care in an assisted living facility. While a wholesaler might be lucky enough to trip into one of these scenarios, they are most often found through a real estate agent.

> <u>Mark-It</u>: **When money becomes urgent, the sales price and transaction time benefit the buyer.**

In these cases, it's like any other sale; the agent lists it, calls people like me, and sells it quickly. From my perspective, the agent's role minimizes the competition as well as the complications.

CHAPTER 16

Wholesalers, Opportunists & Potential Swindlers

In the rehab business, you may encounter wholesalers who broker quick turnovers of distressed properties. Wholesalers aren't necessarily flippers or rehabbers; they buy property to create inventory and make money. You've seen the signs everywhere. These opportunists advertise wherever they can find human eyes: on signs, TV, and more. Designed to grab attention, their campaigns are created by local entrepreneurs who usually attach themselves to a national franchise.

Wholesalers cast a big net. These companies deploy an army of people to search for sellers who are willing to deal below market value. They read obituaries, stand on the courthouse steps, attend auctions, and go door to door to identify cases where mortgages are underwater or properties need to sell quickly. They scour public records to "rescue" people in desperate situations before the bank beats them to the punch. Sniffing out pre-foreclosures that show up on Zillow as soon as one mortgage payment is missed, they seem predatory by nature.

Let's say Mrs. Smith passes away, leaving an estate to her children. In severe disrepair, the home has needs that exceed the time and expertise of the heirs. Knowing that the mortgage has been paid off, the children plan to liquidate the house and close the estate. Since they live outside the area, they consider using a local wholesaler to facilitate the process.

Connections occur in one of two ways. Either an heir will respond to a wholesaler's promotion or the process works in reverse and the company will find the family in need. After adding Mrs. Smith's property to its catalogue, the wholesaler pings a participating investor group of financiers with the goal of creating a match. Once a connection is made, the wholesaler will offer the family a rock-bottom sales price, guaranteeing to buy the house and all its contents for that amount—no frills, no need to clean out the rooms. The offered price is likely to be significantly below market value, near the 50% mark, right out of the chute.

That's only the beginning. Since the wholesaler is in business to make money, the offer will also include a fee, usually about 10% of the sales price. As a middleman between the buyer/investor and seller, it is the wholesaler's job to transfer the property below market price with that 10% built in. A good wholesaler invests a fair amount of money in advertising and research and should, of course, be paid. Yet, 10% is a big chunk of change, so Mrs. Smith's heirs should not be afraid to discuss options before agreeing to an amount. Remember, everything in real estate is negotiable.

A wholesaler never actually owns the property. With a match made, the two parties will enter into a binding contract based on the agreed-upon amount facilitated by the wholesaler. Since the contract is between the buyer/investor and seller, the wholesaler never owns the property. That means the wholesaler doesn't borrow any funds, put money into the project, or incur any fees or transfer taxes. The process is handled in what is commonly known as a double settlement. In most cases, The wholesaler simply settles on the property first—functioning somewhat like a loan—with paperwork that immediately transfers it to the buyer/investor at the settlement that follows. In another method, the original house sale is assigned to the wholesaler and then reassigned to the buyer/investor with no purchase involved. Similar to the double settlement, the wholesaler never actually owns the house but merely assigns it at a higher rate with the fee built in.

Don't pay someone to do your Googling. By hiring a wholesaler, you are basically agreeing to pay for a book of properties that you could probably find on any real estate listing service. The Internet is jam-packed with sites like Zillow that provide anyone with direct access to foreclosures, homes for sale by owner (FSBOs), and more. As you can see, by using wholesalers, people often give away money unnecessarily. While the property changes hands multiple times, significant money is skimmed off before the heirs or sellers are paid.

> **Mark-It**: As a rehab investor, I can accomplish the same outcome at a better value for the seller by acquiring it directly without a middleman.

Seek transparency. In our example, if the heirs had simply sold the home through a qualified real estate agent, they would have paid 5% to 6%—instead of 10% to 20%—for a more thorough and transparent experience. I should say translucent experience, because nothing is truly transparent in the real estate industry. At times, wholesalers can be downright opaque.

It's all about the relationship. Perturbed by the nonsense some wholesalers create, my perceptions run hot and cold. Never owning or creating anything, with the ability to disappear at any time, their business model doesn't seem sustainable. A wholesaler could sell two houses, make $20,000 and do nothing for months on end until the need for money again arises.

The role of wholesalers will become less important to your business after you have established your own connections through genuine experiences. I've had the greatest success in finding valuable properties through real estate agents, saving me the extra fee and enhancing my overall rehab budget. With this said, it may make sense to maintain relationships with a few proven wholesalers you can trust to deliver a good deal. If you're as particular about projects as I am, this affiliation could come in handy when you're in a lull with nothing on the horizon. Good projects are hard to find, and a trusted wholesaler functions as another dedicated scout on your search team.

Never say never. Read on before you jump in. While a few wholesalers still call me with potential properties, I have yet to make a purchase that way. No, wait ... I did buy one property through a wholesaler and it was dreadful. It took over a year to settle from the time I made the deal. Why so long? Remember, the wholesaler doesn't truly own the property, so things can quagmire to the point where the whole deal falls apart. This story is actually more of a nightmare. Although getting the property to settlement was an ordeal, I can't really blame the wholesaler. The unusual situation made it impossible for anyone to resolve.

Early in my rehab career, a wholesaler notified me about a two-story house in a desirable neighborhood. Inhabited by squatters for a short time, it was on the market through a bank repossession. The property piqued my interest because the price was right, calculated at about 55% of its value. I knew I'd need to come up with quick cash because the seller wanted to close in 30 days. Since I would be borrowing money from a lender, I planned to coordinate the transactions to avoid paying interest on a property that wasn't in my control.

When I visited the site I noticed that the area around the windows was overgrown, blocking my view inside. Upon entering the house and making sure the electricity was turned off, I went to the basement and found a horrid sight. Random belongings were floating in muck: slimy furniture, mushy boxes, and soaked clothes. Wearing a mask, I surveyed rooms that had grown black and musty. Although the structure was relatively new, I could see that the water issues had originated from overflowing gutters and a broken sump pipe. Clearly those were problems, but they were ones I could fix. Despite a basement submerged in water, I was 99.9% sure these issues were repairable.

On the main level, excess moisture was causing the hardwood floors to cup, and mold was creeping into dark corners. Someone had broken into the back window, which was exposed again after being boarded up. The house needed attention—quickly.

After completing the site visit and conducting my due diligence, I signed an agreement stipulating that I'd buy the house from the wholesaler when he settled on it. To prepare for this, I needed to have money available to close in one month. Within five days I had presented the deal to my lender, received agreement, and acquired access to the funding needed.

Meanwhile, my real estate agent was working on my behalf. His research showed that the original owner who foreclosed on the property was still listed on the deed. This created a problem in transferring the property because the bank that claimed ownership was not referenced. My agent and I continued to monitor the parcel knowing we could not proceed with closing until we had a deed showing the bank as the rightful owner. Finding ourselves in this unusual situation, we continued to push for answers as the settlement date came and went.

At that point, I found myself in a stressful lending situation because I had paid more points than I should have to get the money quickly. My first interest payment was due at the end of the month with no closing in sight. To make matters worse, part of the lender's rationale for loaning me the money was based on him receiving a lienholder position on the property. With the unresolved deed issue, I couldn't even execute the final loan documents from the lender because I didn't have a property to put them on.

I now had unsecured money hanging in limbo on a property that the person offering it could not sell. Another month went by and we still didn't have the glimmer of a settlement date. It was a classic catch-22. I was supposed to be nimble and ready to go on a moment's notice, yet I had no idea when the property could settle. I had no choice but to give the money back to the lender with a promise that the loan would settle quickly when I got a clear title on the other end.

This debacle cost me nothing but money for months. Constantly, I had to be ready with $150,000 in hand, not counting the money I would need for the rehab. Finally, I tied up cash of my own to avoid defaulting on the contract and losing the property. Meanwhile, I became interested in a second property that I secured with a different investor in order to remain ready to close with the first lender when the deed issue was resolved.

Of course I could have cancelled the contract on the first property but I was unwilling to lose an attractive project to someone who would swoop in as soon as the title issue was resolved. As a result, I kept renewing and extending the contract for almost a year while the house continued to decline. After the title issues were finally resolved, I reduced my offer and the accompanying loan based on the fact that the house had deteriorated significantly. When I was finally able to start work, I had lost most of the hardwood floors and sheetrock on the main level along with just about everything in the basement. I had a major project on my hands but got through it. Spending a bit more than planned, I rehabbed the property and

115

sold it at the first open house.

In the end, it turned out to be a nice little project with a nice little profit. But it could have been a disaster. And, for a while, it was. The point is that a lot of nonsense kept me from being flexible enough to purchase the properties I needed for my ongoing rehab work. Cash flow is key in this business, and when it's tied up in uncontrollable situations, it becomes a problem. If you decide to venture into this world, be cautious and don't sign anything until a professional real estate agent assesses the property. Trust me, it's worth it. And "trust me" is exactly what the wholesaler will say, right before you hand over the money. Get control whenever you can.

CHAPTER 17

Networking, Socializing, Meetings & Other Excuses to Drink and Play Golf

There's no better way to sum up my discussion on finding properties than to highlight the most important ingredient: real estate agents. From the standpoint of pricing, opportunity, clean contracts, and limited competition, nothing beats working with a Realtor. The process will be less complicated, the timeframe shorter, and fewer people will be involved. With a goal of getting the best property with the smoothest timeline at the cheapest price, real estate agents are the way to make this happen.

These professionals truly make a difference. As a rehabber, the most effective way to find the unique properties I'm looking for is by networking but that takes time. Perhaps they're good at pretending, but real estate agents always seem to have time. They socialize, meet, learn, drink, and laugh. If they sometimes look like big-time partiers, it's all a ploy. They're really networking.

This is why I spend a big chunk of my money on real estate agents. Of course there are marketing fees and commissions, but my most valuable investment is in networking. I buy drinks, schedule lunches, host golf outings, throw parties, and create as many reasons as possible to interact with these professionals.

> **Mark-It**: **Money spent on agent networking is an investment that pays back many times over. In addition to helping me find properties, agents connect me to valuable business leaders, planning and zoning officials, settlement attorneys, and more.**

These connections have been invaluable when I have needed them the most. The real estate industry is known for surprises. It takes a network of people to help you stay ahead of the game. Armed with tools to help you find properties and navigate the closing process, agents are the people who make things happen. Best of all, they won't turn down a party, event, or any reason to tip back a drink or two.

My reciprocal relationship with the Garceau team and my agent Dale has created untold benefits, including access to an office, copiers, advice, and marketing tools. Best of all, they know buyers—a lot of them. I can't tell you how many properties I've sold on word of mouth and never had to market because of my partnership with real estate agents. And yes, I pay full commission in those situations because their service helps me every day.

There are many ways to find distressed properties, and the best opportunities flow through a real estate agent whether they come from local listings or online auctions. I can attribute most of my success in this business to the professionals I've been blessed to know. Smart and authentic, they have a work ethic that is balanced by a sense of humor I can't live without. I rely on these people for marketing, advice, and networking. Most importantly, they make this business entertaining, worthwhile, and—when times are tough—tolerable.

PART FOUR

THE LIVING, BREATHING STRUCTURE

Rehabbing is filled with mistakes and triumphs.
I've had my share of both.
I hope mine inspire you to create some of your own.

WARNING: Read this part at your own risk.

It's filled with things I've learned about houses from eight years of college, 30 years of experience, and a lifetime of trying. You'll soon see ...
    I'm not a master electrician,
    I'm not a professional plumber,
    I'm not an expert roofer,
    I'm not a landscaping architect
... but, thank God, I've learned from the best of them.

Since this part deals with the meat and potatoes of home construction, you may decide to read Part Five first. But you don't want to skip this section altogether. As MacGyver taught us, sometimes survival depends on tips, tricks, and a whole lot of duct tape.

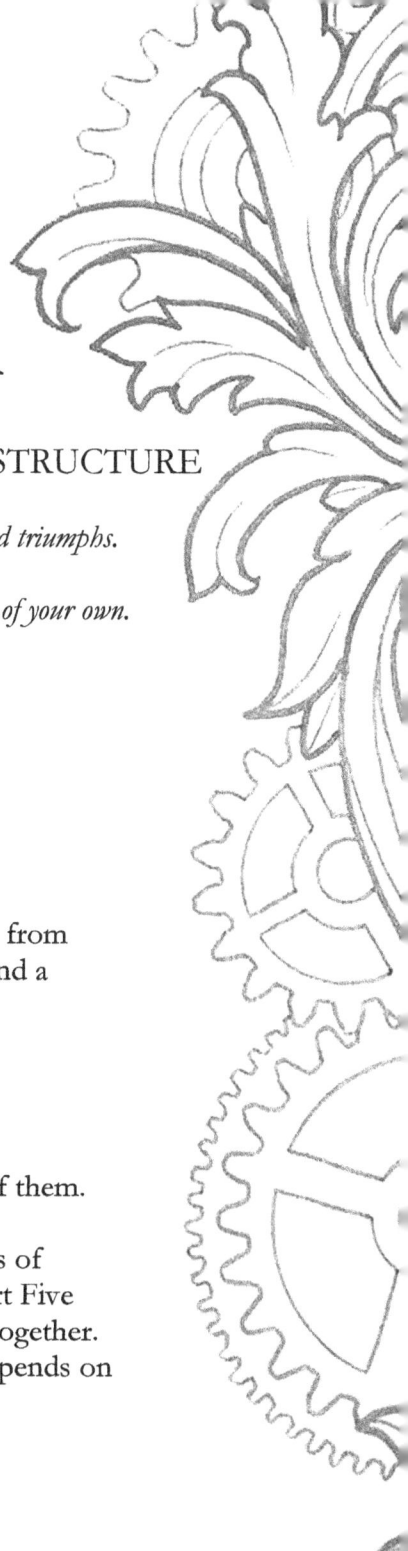

CHAPTER 18

It's What's on the Outside That Counts

When it comes to houses, everyone is excited about what lies beyond the front door. But, if the outside isn't right, chances are people will drive right past and never find all the goodness inside. As rehabbers, our job is to create an exterior that keeps them wanting more.

Research before you renovate. Removing and replacing exterior materials can eat up your entire budget so don't do that unless you know it's necessary. Review the property, hop on your computer, and learn as much as possible so you can deliver a functional, durable, appealing outer shell. Before you tear the siding off, here's a checklist:

1) Note the period when the house was built
2) Look at the existing materials
3) Understand how they were installed
4) Assess how they were maintained
5) Research current product advancements

Let's say you have a 1920s house with stone or brick exterior that has withstood the elements for 100 years. If these thick, well-insulated materials were installed over solid sheathing and durable framing—and maintained correctly—they could last forever, and a few chipped sections are fairly easy to repair. On the other hand, a clapboard exterior is less forgiving. Without proper sealing to keep water and insects out, the wood becomes increasingly susceptible to termites, weather, and dry rot. Plan to remove wood products that contain evidence of mold or insect damage. The same strategy applies if you uncover plywood treated with formaldehyde. Do your assessment. Know what you have.

The elephant in the room: asbestos. Contrary to popular belief, asbestos is one of the most incredible manmade products ever created. It's fire retardant, a good insulator, easy to work with, and long lasting. Because of these performance characteristics, asbestos was used on many houses from the 1940s to the 1960s.

If you encounter a house with asbestos siding, it doesn't mean the seller is a shyster as long as the product has been well-maintained and properly disclosed. If it is in good condition, asbestos siding can often be painted and kept in place. With this said, be aware that retaining asbestos—even in pristine condition—may become a deterrent to resale because the general population has been trained to think it is always dangerous. Despite the product's performance benefits, buyers will run in the opposite direction at the mere mention of the word "asbestos."

Here's what you need to know. If it's not handled properly—primarily at installation or demolition—asbestos can and does cause cancer. The problem arises when a person works with it day after day, cutting and breaking it in an unventilated area without proper protection. Before these dangers were discovered, it was common for workers to spray asbestos insulation and breathe in hazardous dust particles that may have contributed to serious illnesses.

> <u>Mark-It</u>: **When you encounter a house with asbestos, be diligent, learn what you are dealing with, and follow safety procedures as you determine the best way forward.**

While it is important to understand the hazards of asbestos and use proper handling techniques, we are sometimes subjected to an uninformed environment of fear. It's interesting to see how this works.

Ten people can die in car accidents at a single corner, yet no one bans cars. When these things happen, everyone works to make cars safer by adding seat belts, no-lock brakes, and more. The world of construction is different. When a problem arises, the first solution is usually a product ban. Asbestos products might have been viewed differently if we had worked to make them better and safer, but that's not how it went.

The inside scoop on outside stuff. When it comes to exterior materials, today's workhorses are vinyl or a fiber cement siding such as HardiPlank. These high-performing products often allow you to skip the headache of removing existing materials since they can be installed over just about anything. Offering a variety of texture, color, and optional features, they are ideal for creating many popular façades.

While both products will enhance the home's value with a cost-effective, fresh look, they have their differences. Paintable and easy to repair, fiber cement siding is the better insulator and will last longer. However, this composite material is more expensive to buy and install.

Vinyl is cheaper but fades over time, and older versions will need to be replaced. The most challenging issue with vinyl siding is its tendency to become brittle and break, especially in cold climates. To make matters worse, replacement is difficult. When a piece of vinyl is damaged by flying debris from a lawnmower, it is challenging to remove and repair it without damaging the adjacent layers. If the repair is successful, your next concern is whether the color of your newly-installed piece will blend with the weathered product on the house. Vinyl siding can be revived with special paint but it must be re-applied every five to seven years. Thankfully, some of the newer vinyl materials are more fade-resistant.

In developing the exterior strategy for a home rehab, focus on the end user and determine where you will get the most bang for your buck. Buyers with deep pockets may prefer fiber cement, stone, or brick for a low-maintenance, long-lasting exterior. If you plan to add new product on an entire house, opt for vinyl to accommodate the budgets of cost-conscious buyers.

Mark-It: When cost is an issue, use brick, stone, or fiber cement in small areas for impact. For example, install fiber cement shell-style shingles in the gable of a Victorian façade for a reliable insulator with added appeal.

In addition to the materials I've mentioned, you may encounter metal or aluminum siding on older homes. Once popular, these exterior materials are no longer desired and should be replaced. Metal siding looks horrible and fades even more than its vinyl counterpart. It is easily dinged and dented, and nearly impossible to repair. All it takes is an errant baseball, rock, or branch, and metal siding will never look smooth and new again. In addition to being noisy and cold, metal is a poor insulator. Think about your Moscow mule mug. It's not an insulator; it's a conductor. If you come across aluminum siding, budget for a replacement. Unlike a Moscow mule, no one wants it.

CHAPTER 19

Windows, Doors & Other Holes in the Wall

Creating an inviting exterior is only the first step in getting people through the door. Of course, there's the door itself. Whether it is new or restored, the front door has to be right. The humans who inhabit the house will come home to this door every day. They'll look at it, touch it, and bring cherished people, pets, and belongings through it. It's the first impression, the focal point.

You may choose to replace or restore the front door, but if it is a classic relic in period style, I can't overemphasize the value of preserving it for future generations. Once you've decided on a plan, take a look at the home's other entryways, including sliding glass doors. Doors may have missing glass, broken panels, and other damage that requires replacement. You can keep ancillary doors made of steel, insulated wood, or vinyl that are functional and in good condition.

> **Mark-It: When it comes to doors, identify the keepers and replace old styles that are non-functional, dented, or difficult to operate.**

Garage doors are often seen as merely utilitarian, yet they play a significant role in a home's exterior appeal. Old-fashioned garage doors can immediately date a house and undermine an otherwise appealing exterior. Relatively inexpensive compared with other house updates, garage door replacement is usually a good investment. Not only will this improve the home's aesthetic appeal, it may help you avoid one more inspection headache.

Find a flipper's telltale signs. If you're the buyer of a restored home, the garage door is a good way to gauge your rehabber. A dated, mediocre garage door may be the first sign of a flipper who tried to cut corners. The same holds true for shutters and other exterior features.

> **Mark-It: A home's exterior sets the tone for what is inside. Deficiencies in these areas may signal other problems. Look for a rehabber who sweats the details**.

Look *at* the windows before you look through them. Windows represent one of the most complicated and important elements in a home. As a rehabber, your window decisions will be time-consuming and house-specific. Check everything and ask these questions:

1) Do the windows open *and* close easily?
2) Are they an efficient, economic value for the new homeowner?
3) Do they help with controlling the home's interior comfort?

Given the importance of windows, I employ an expert to inspect every opening for issues such as condition, function, and clouding.

> **Mark-It: Develop a repair vs. replacement cost threshold and stick with it. If estimated repairs will exceed your threshold, replace the windows and start over.**

There is no need to replace windows just because they are 15-20 years old as long as they are in good working order and integral to the house style. Newer versions may have insulated glass with no storm windows while old styles are the exact opposite. Either approach may be acceptable depending on the window condition, but steer clear of unattractive styles that date the house. Even high-end windows will need to be replaced if they are dysfunctional with brittle seals and broken glass. Most modern homes have vinyl-clad windows that are easy to replace, adding value your buyers will appreciate.

Windows give a house its attitude. When it comes to windows, keeping an authentic feature is often more important than adding a new product. If your project is a period house characterized by unique windows—a colonial, craftsman or farmhouse, for example—then restore them. No matter how hard you try, you'll never replicate the genuine character of an English Tudor's original diamond windows with leaded glass. By attempting to change the windows, you're likely to alter the look of the house, and not in a good way.

> **Mark-It: When I come across cool features such as farmhouse glass, old glazing, and original leaded designs, I preserve them and add storm windows if needed. While preservation may cost as much as replacement, there is usually greater value in maintaining genuine features.**

A screen can be a window's worst nightmare. I've encountered a recurring problem in some homes with double-hung windows. Even though the window design includes small brackets that make the screens easy to remove, people tend to leave them in year-round, unleashing a vicious cycle.

First, the glass becomes extremely dirty from bugs, pollen, dirt, and more. With the screen on the outside, the glass is never fully rinsed by seasonal rains, allowing dirt, pollen, and mud to build up between the outside of the window and the inside of the screen. Over time, a paste of dirt and gunk forms at the bottom of the window, often becoming ½-inch thick or more. Once this paste settles in, the sun comes out, dries things up, and makes the gunk as hard as concrete. The concrete gunk then creates a seal, cementing the screen to the window sill. What happens the next time it rains? If the homeowner is lucky, the gunk breaks up and dirty water oozes from the bottom of the window on the outside. But, in most cases, it wreaks havoc. Held by a cement layer of gunk, water collects against the screen, filling the bottom of the window sill all the way to the height of the screen's frame. This swimming pool in the window sill causes the wood to rot until the water eventually finds its way inside the house.

When a situation like this is left unresolved for months or years, it will destroy the sill, ruin the windows, and create additional damage inside the house. Wooden sashes can be sanded and repaired, but often the

126

only remedy is window replacement. I've had to do this more times than I cared to, all because mindless people didn't remove their screens. Thankfully, new screen technology in modern windows has remedied this situation but there are still plenty of these problems out there in the rehab world. If you have the older window/screen configuration, do yourself a favor and avoid this catastrophe.

Mark-It: In my opinion, window screens detract from a home's exterior appeal, so I remove them from the front of my rehabbed houses. Realizing that new owners and home inspectors may not agree with my perspective, I store them in the basement for later use, but I've never been asked to reinstall them.

Style matters. For interior doors, choose styles that match the home you are rehabbing. Whether it is a craftsman, industrial, farmhouse, or something else, the products and hardware you select are essential to the home's overall aesthetics. While I typically replace dated styles such as flush or 6-panel, vintage doors are making a comeback in variations that include 3-panel, 5-panel and shaker designs.

Doors and windows create a first impression—and people see them every day—so don't grab the first thing you see at the nearest big box store. Be selective, choosing products that will enhance the home's character.

CHAPTER 20

It's More Than a Roof Over Your Head

I'm a firm believer that a roof is much more than a functional cover. Together with a variety of exterior elements that define a home's quality, colors, and texture, it communicates curb appeal.

Shape and Style

There are many roof styles, such as lean-to, sloped, and gable, and many were designed to save costs. Popular on Dutch colonials, the gambrel or barn-style roof extended over the second floor to minimize the volume of expensive brick product.

> **Mark-it**: Although I love Dutch colonials, my broker insists that most people dislike the style so I keep that in mind when I'm looking at houses to rehab. What do you think? Am I the crazy one, or is she?

Another distinct roof style is mansard, shaped like a tent with four sloping sides, each bending to a point. These roofs often feature a widow's walk, which evolved as a place for a sea captain's wife to pace at the peak as she watched for her husband's return. Accommodating a square-shaped house, this style may also include other details or railings. While these decorative features add character to the house, the flat orientation of a mansard roof makes it prone to leaks and more difficult to maintain.

Many mid-century modern homes were designed with flat roofs that relied on summer heat to seal the asphalt surface for the duration of the seasons. If you take on a mid-century modern project with a flat roof, be sure to inspect it and follow up to ensure there are no leaks. With this type of roof, sloped areas in the tar help to divert water into drains that run along the interior of the building or around the outside cornice. On smaller roofs, water is directed to specific overhangs. Today, flat roofs are most prevalent on commercial buildings since they provide a cost-effective way to cover longer spans.

Form and Function

A roof's shape is defined by trusses that are stick-built or manufactured. To add durability and prevent water infiltration, trusses are covered with ¾-inch plywood that is connected by tabs at the corners and edges. This technique was sufficient for several years, until tornados and hurricanes lifted entire peaks off their structures. Now, metal straps are used to fasten the trusses to the walls, providing extra support in heavy winds. With the plywood and straps in place, a thick, black tar or felt paper is applied to further guard against leaks. Shingles are then layered on top, starting at the bottom and working upward so the nails are always covered to avoid water infiltration.

Early roofs were covered with a variety of materials that provided water barriers, including thatch or layers of straw. Since these materials rotted and leaked over time, frequent replacements were required, ushering in sturdier products such as stone, slate, and cedar shake. Although durable, these heavier products required a stronger structure to carry the extra weight. Cedar shakes also tended to dry out, split, crack, and leak, making them a challenge to maintain.

Today, architectural asphalt shingles provide both form and function, offering transitions in color and texture to beautify the house. There are a variety of styles and patterns, with rough-cut splits that convey the look of shake or slate. With a 25- to 30-year warranty, these roofing materials are typically comprised of a rubber membrane glued over a dense, foam insulation. Low-end, 3-tab shingles offering a 20-year warranty are also available. Thinner and more susceptible to wind damage, these inferior shingles provide little intrinsic value and are not recommended. As you encounter projects with older roof products, be aware that some tar materials will leak and may be expensive to restore, making this a losing effort.

> **Mark-It**: **If you purchase a historic house with a slate or shake roof, I recommend keeping the product if the materials are in good condition. While repairing these types of roofs can be costly, it is worth the expense to preserve natural elements that will stand the test of time and enhance the home's value.**

Breathe and Vent

As a living, breathing structure, a house requires air, so a roof overview would not be complete without a discussion of attic and ridge vents. Since air is the best insulator, a nicely ventilated upper pocket will shield rooms below and prevent a build-up of moisture and humidity. Attic vents have long been a preferred way to send in cool, fresh air and draw out hot, old air via a small electric fan. As new roof technology evolves, these attic fans are being replaced by ridge vents. Instead of requiring a mechanical apparatus that must be turned on to generate air movement, the ridge vent uses a natural process.

Ridge vents are formed when the roofer cuts the plywood at the top of the gable, leaving a 3-inch gap that extends along the length of the house. The roofing material is then installed up to the edge of this opening without covering it. When the roof is completed, special shingles, or ridge vents, are added at the top. These ridge vents replaced the older, metal styles that often blew off in high winds, allowing water to enter the attic. The modern version is a composite ridge vent, which is a piece of dense, breathable foam that functions like a sponge to allow air through. Designed in a color to match the shingles on the roof, it is laid on top to create a smooth, curved "A" shape at the peak. Spacer nails are used to ensure a proper gap without allowing water to run into the house. Easy to spot in new communities, these ridge vents eliminate costly maintenance while letting nature handle the air circulation process.

Assess and Inspect

Check the condition of all roofing materials to ensure that each piece is in place and the insulation meets code. Getting this right will make a big difference in utility costs for the future homeowner. If roof repairs or replacements are needed, they are typically easy and cost-effective if you identify them early in the process.

> **Mark-It**: **Your roof inspection should include a focus on the L-shaped metal flashing that seals the connection points at curves and 90-degree angles near chimneys and walls.**

When it is attached to natural brick or stone, flashing appears as a stairstep pattern, layered in sections that are finished with caulk. In most cases, flashing on an older home will need to be replaced with a modern, pliable, metal product. Older styles that were made of copper or other expensive metals may be maintained if they are in good condition but should be re-caulked when the roof is addressed. Be sure to check the entire house for dried, cracking caulk and replace it to avoid future leaks.

Finally, inspect the eaves, overhangs, and gutter systems for signs of clogging or sagging. Downspouts and eaves rely on gravity to effectively move water away from the house and must be repositioned as needed to ensure proper flow. There is nothing worse than overflowing gutters or eaves with an incorrect fall dumping rainwater near a home's foundation and subjecting it to long-term water damage.

> **Mark-It**: **I recommend the use of seamless gutters, fresh cut by a machine on site, rather than an off-the-shelf, seamed version that will eventually leak and cause damage.**

Roof, roof. Got it? Okay, I'll stop barking at you.

CHAPTER 21

It's a Basement, Not a Boat

People think of basements as home theaters, kids' playrooms, or man caves. Truth is, that's not what basements are. That's what people *turned basements into*. A basement is actually the living, breathing structural foundation for a house. How did this essential building block end up performing double duty as living space? And where does water come into play ... literally? To answer these questions, let's start by looking behind—and below—the basement walls.

Underneath every home lies a frost line, the point at which the ground above could freeze solid. Building a footer above that line would put a home at serious risk of being heaved upward by the incredible pressure of freezing, expanding water. Sound impossible? Think about what happens when the pilings for a boat pier are installed at an inferior depth. Over time, the pilings—and the pier—will be pushed upward when the ground water freezes and expands with unyielding force. A house is no different. Same water. Same powerful expansion. Same upward motion.

Now that we've established where to begin, let's focus on how a basement comes together. The foundation begins with the footer, which is dug in a consistent, level trench below the frost line. Seen from above, this trench is an outline in the earth, defining the shape of the house and providing the first glimpse of what it will become. The completed trench will be filled with concrete 10 to 12 inches deep and 12 to 20 inches wide, depending on the code requirements for stability in various climates.

With the footer in place, the foundation walls begin to take shape, providing the structure that will carry the weight of the house through time and change. The walls are laid on top of the footer with rebar added to link the elements. At this point, water prevention strategies are implemented to provide a moisture barrier and divert water away from the foundation before the area around the exterior walls is filled in and graded.

In the earliest days, foundation walls—and sometimes the footer itself—were crafted from available materials such as stacked stones or bricks held together with mortar best described as glorified mud made of limestone and water. While today's foundation walls are often constructed of concrete block or poured concrete, they are still quite porous—just like their predecessors.

And that brings us to water.

Water is persistent. When it rains, water penetrates the ground. Dig a hole, and it eventually fills with water. There's no way around it. That's why we cover basements with a house and a roof. Otherwise, they would fill with water and become ponds. A basement is never going to float. And, regardless of what it says on the side of a company truck, a basement will not be completely waterproof.

Because it's a basement, not a boat.

The first basements were typically about 6 or 7 feet tall with dirt floors that were sometimes loosely paved with scattered bricks. This was not a living space and it was not intended to be controlled in any way. There in the cellar, flowing water was common, with channels created to direct streams through the space and into a drain or pit.

The basement remained as unused space until its owners began to view it differently. The underground positioning meant that a basement maintained a consistent temperature in the mid-60s, making it the perfect place for storing fruits, vegetables, supplies, coal, heating fuel, and more. The space soon evolved into a summer kitchen with a cooking hearth converted from the brick base that supported the fireplace in the home above.

It didn't stop there. In warmer climates, families realized that the cool environment was the ideal space for relaxing after chores, sleeping during sweltering summer nights, and finding protection from storms. As the years rolled on, furniture was added, the floor was dug deeper, mechanicals were housed there, and the space became finished. The rest is history.

Today, that cozy family space is still assembled from a porous wall attached to a porous footer. It seals up fairly well, but regardless of how effectively we attach these two permeable elements, we can't assume that the connection will be waterproof. So, when we put these concrete structures into the ground and the water has no place to go, it might just end up in the basement.

Because it's a basement, not a boat.

Now we know the real truth. Based on their underground location, basements are inclined to be cool and damp. While we can't entirely waterproof a basement, there is a lot we can do to divert the moisture away. Before determining how to proceed, we need to identify where the water sneaks in. Let's talk about the main causes of water infiltration and what we can do to address each one.

1- Ground Water Runoff

Ground water runoff occurs when the earth becomes saturated from a variety of sources, such as heavy rain or overflowing gutters and downspouts. In these cases, a deluge may be dumped next to the foundation, soaking through the porous walls. Common evidence of this issue is the appearance of dampness on the foundation wall at a height equal to the backfill around the house. In block wall structures, you might notice a white powdery residue from chemicals in the mortar that leach in with the water.

Mark-It: **A major culprit of ground water runoff is improper grading, especially common with older homes.**

Ideally, a home should be positioned at the property's highest elevation. If the ground is sloped toward the house in any location, a swale will cause water to collect against the foundation. Often, this problem is compounded over time because plants and mulch beds camouflage the issue until it becomes critical. It can be costly, too, since ground water runoff claims may not be covered by insurance.

Grading issues are easily avoided during the construction process if proper procedures are followed. When the foundation is dug, the disturbed area around the house should be narrow, keeping the ground as stable as possible. If fill dirt is added, it could take years for the soil to settle into the area, impacting the grade. A properly graded space covered with vegetation will move water at least 3 to 4 feet away from the house, channeling rainfall as if it is running on concrete.

Additional water mitigation techniques include installing a sealant or membrane to wrap the foundation wall or adding a French drain system to collect and divert water. These methods are merely deterrents that will eventually wear down and require repair so they should be used only to support proper grading procedures.

2- Subterranean Water

Subterranean water exists in a variety of forms that may not be discovered until excavation is already underway. This hidden water may be an underground stream or a pocket of moisture pushing up in a specific area.

Mark-It: **Be sure to identify and address underground water issues early in the process because correcting them later is far more expensive.**

In existing homes, we may learn that a layer of water is running up against the bottom of the foundation, or that hydrostatic pressure is pushing upward below the slab. In these cases, there will be evidence of water coming in around the lower corners of the basement, sometimes with minimal absorption seeping up the walls. This underground pressure may compromise the slab, causing it to crack in one or more locations, often with water creeping in along the fractures.

Some geographic areas do not provide favorable conditions for building basements due to sandy soils and coastal, low-lying landscapes. Despite the circumstances, you may encounter homes in these regions that were built with basements due to customer demand.

In all cases, I recommend taking steps to avoid subterranean water issues *before* the slab is poured. First, install a system of drains to divert water away from the structure and into a sump pit. Dig a trench around the perimeter walls, just above the top of the footer. This trench will be filled with a series of corrugated pipes that are sloped to collect water over time, like gutters and downspouts. Gravel is then added to protect the pipes when the slab is poured. All of these pipes work together, from one end of the house to the other, channeling water into concrete-lined sump pits that will ultimately collect it, keeping moisture out of the basement.

Later, the slab will be installed in a continuous pour over a layer of gravel, sand, and rebar before being smoothed and finished. A slight gap is left between the edge of the slab and the foundation wall, providing a pathway to guide emerging water into the drain system. The gap is accomplished by adding pieces of plywood or plastic inserts around the walls before the slab is poured, leaving a ¼-inch space between the edge of the wall. This is an important part of the diversion system to ensure that any water coming into the basement from ground water runoff, subterranean issues, or other means will find its way to the edges of the slab, down the drain tiles, and over to the pits.

Now that the slab is in and our drain tiles and pits have been installed, it's time to add the pump. The sump pump is an underwater mechanism that sits on the bottom of the pit with an attached float to turn the switch on and off, similar to the float in a toilet. On the sump pump, an electric switch stops the pump as the water drops down and turns it on as the water rises.

Keep in mind that the water being channeled through the system exerts tremendous pressure. Think of holding your finger over a straw in a glass of water and then raising it. As soon as you let go, the water comes out of the straw. A sump pump operates the same way. It pumps water up the pipe (straw), and when the pump turns off, the water pushes back into the pit. We use a backflow preventer or check valve to manage this process. Functioning much like the flapper in the bottom of a toilet tank, it allows the weight of the water to seal the valve as needed. While this device plays an important role, it is common to find homes where it is missing or broken.

A pipe extends from the sump pump, running above ground level, through the foundation wall, and out into the yard. This pipe is directed away from the house—preferably 3 to 5 feet—and an additional underground channel with pop-up drain may be used to extend the water farther if necessary.

This drain system process represents one of our best opportunities to keep water away from the house and avoid future runoff issues. Without a concentrated water diversion plan, there is a greater potential for moisture to find its way back into the basement in an endless cycle. Remember, we are not waterproofing the basement—we are diverting water away from it.

3- House-Generated Issues

Many water problems are not the result of outside infiltration, coming instead from sources within the house itself. These types of issues may involve plumbing glitches, burst pipes, roof leaks, mechanical challenges, and more. Anything that is connected to a pressurized water system and left unchecked—such as an icemaker or a dishwasher hose—can cause a nightmare of water problems. Once a leak occurs, water eventually will fall to the lowest point in the house where it may sit in darkness over time, leading to mold, wood rot, and expensive repairs.

Mark-It: I've found that about 90% of water issues are house-generated.

For example, when a home is not properly winterized, pipes freeze and expand, and the PVC or copper gives way under pressure. Because the water is still on, it continues to flow. If this occurs in an upstairs bathroom, water will fall several floors and ultimately land in the basement, creating a lot of structural damage along the way.

When it comes to leaks, broken pipes are common culprits. In abandoned houses, the power or water may be turned off, aggravating the problem and making identification more difficult.

Mark-It: My strategy is to first identify the sources of water problems before investigating the pipes.

Once a plumbing issue has been determined, I can turn on the water to find and correct the problem. Unlike the basement, a home's upper levels do not naturally maintain a constant temperature, so broken pipes often occur in these areas. Upon discovering the source of the problem, I search the rooms below for damage to floors and ceilings in the water's path. Even if the water has been turned off, this type of evidence is usually easy to identify.

Mechanical systems create an additional opportunity for water problems, and upper-level laundry rooms are notorious contributors. Water from pressurized laundry tubs left unattended, failing washing machines, or faulty water tanks can deliver a deluge of damage. Consider the potential impact of a hot water tank with a rusted bottom that eventually gives way. In this case, the extent of impact is dependent upon the location of the tank and how long power and water are turned on.

Let's move up to the roof. In cases of water infiltration from this area, the first clue is often a stained spot on the ceiling, sometimes with visible water dripping through. Everyone has been there. We grab a bucket to catch the water until the issue can be repaired. In abandoned houses, this issue could linger for years. The stained

138

spot on the ceiling expands, saturates the insulation, and seeps into the sheetrock. With no one there to grab a bucket and repair the problem, the weight of the soaked sheetrock and insulation eventually collapses into the room below. This launches a series of chain reactions that continue downward until the saturated mess finds its way into the basement. Creating devastating damage, roof leaks often leave rotted wood, mold, and other problems in their wake. They start at the top of the house and work their way downward, damaging everything that gets in the way.

Identifying problems and resolving them are two different things, and in a vacant house, they may be easy or difficult. The path of destruction makes roof leaks simple to identify, with resolutions that require roof replacement or repair. Yet, other types of moisture problems may hide when water and power are not active. In a public system, if the water flow has been terminated following a leak, it often requires extensive investigative work to fully identify the damage. On a well system, the sump pump may eventually burn out and fail due to the constant flow of water from a neglected leak. Occasionally, the power has been shut off but the water is still on, creating a worst-case scenario where the sump pump is not functioning and the water runs endlessly, flooding the basement and potentially turning it into a swimming pool.

Now that we've discussed the physical nature of basements, identified the main sources of water infiltration, and outlined several remedies, it is clear that basements require special attention when it comes to moisture. To combat the natural tendency toward dampness, every basement should be dehumidified in some manner. This may be accomplished through an effective HVAC system with ample vents and returns, or with a standalone dehumidifier that pulls moisture from the air. Basements are porous, concrete structures nestled in the earth, attracting humidity. And, the wetter the climate, the more moisture will find its way in.

Because it's a basement, not a boat.

All this talk of water reminds me of a story about a striking mid-century modern. She was a sleek rancher, circa 1954. A Maryland native, yes, but she was a California girl through and through.

The agent listed the house as a tear-down but after one look you couldn't tear me away. She had remarkable, authentic features. Large plate glass windows, glass blocks, a deco feel, and a low, flat roof with expansive overhangs. She wore a full brick ensemble that fit just right. Super cool.

Sure, she had baggage, but she was full of personality. Her kitchen was horribly outdated, but the stone fireplace was spectacular. Hardwood floors dominated the space, with three bedrooms and two full baths on the main floor. Ahead of her time, she featured a mudroom/laundry area on the main floor off the garage.

Partially finished and carpeted, the basement was being used as storage for boxes, clothes, antiques, and more. There was no dampness, no odor, no moist cardboard, no reason to think this home ever had a water issue.

The home's builder and original owner was a member of the well-known family that owned the surrounding land. While he and his wife lived in a barn on the property, the owner chose the highest point in the area as the site for their future home. His wife had the chance to travel out west where she fell in love with mid-century modern architecture. In fact, she returned so inspired by it that her husband vowed to build their home in that style, a rare sight for this locale.

As best I can tell, he built the home without a plan. No kidding; he winged it. Yet, structurally, you could drop a bomb on the house and it probably wouldn't go anywhere. All brick on a concrete block foundation, it was solid as a rock. The interior walls were an early version of drywall, almost plaster-like, with no wooden slats beneath. At the time, the basement must have been used as a storm cellar. A set of stairs led outside, protected from the elements by the access doors. Another staircase provided direct access from the mudroom to the main living area.

After listening to the home's story and considering her journey through the years, I ventured another look. She was elegantly perched on the highest point in the area with a side porch off the family room that overlooked a golf course. Too cool to be torn down, she had to be saved.

So that's exactly what happened. I went all out, in a painstaking endeavor to honor her mid-century roots. I replaced the old tar roof with a flat, rubber membrane and stylish metal flashing. The windows were exchanged *for new panes with custom-ordered black metal trim to pay homage to the originals. I power washed the brick, removed, replaced, and sealed the glass blocks, and installed new glass garage doors with sleek, black metal framing that mimicked a commercial structure.*

Inside, the open floorplan set the stage for time-honored updates. I tiled the bathrooms, added backlit mirrors, and installed floating vanities. The result was a modern take on mid-century grace accomplished with attention to detail across light fixtures, hardware, and finishes. We respected and preserved existing features such as the built-in bookcase and dining room china cabinet.

With the project nearing completion, I took pictures, sent out invitations, and prepared for our first open house. Knowing that this house would have a very specific niche buyer, I was prepared to sit on it for a while. The day before the event, our area was hit with a ridiculous wind storm that knocked down power poles and trees across the county. It was a debacle. Most of Bel Air was without power.

Debating what to do, my agent Dale and I considered canceling the open house but ultimately decided to move forward. I couldn't shake a nagging need to be there. When we arrived, the signs had blown down but the power was back on. Just before 11:00, we began to turn on all the lights in preparation for one or two guests who might straggle in. As I flipped the switch in the laundry room, I saw a car pull into the driveway. Waiting in the small room, I listened as Dale greeted the prospects. That's how we work—he takes the lead and knows just when to bring me into the conversation to provide explanations, add details, and share stories.

Soon, Dale appeared at the door of the laundry room with a young couple. As he made the introductions, I could tell that the woman was visibly shaken. Without skipping a beat, her husband asked what it would take for us to close the open house, get the property off the market, and finalize the sale. Dale responded, "A full price offer would be a good place to start." Despite all I have seen through the years, I was dumbfounded. Right then and there, the couple called their mortgage broker, gave us a full price offer, and bought a house they hadn't fully toured. In fact, they hadn't left the main floor.

As it turned out, this couple had been living in an apartment, desperately

141

searching for the house of their dreams. Unlike many of the center-stair colonials in our market, this house had a style they were looking for. This house was different from everything they had seen. This house was them.

I thought, "they get it, they love it, they'll care for it. It will be their thing." I couldn't have been happier. The house had found its perfect owners. They moved in, bought things, decorated, and made themselves at home.

And it was good.

Then came the summer of biblical rains. It poured for days on end. I received a text. Lo and behold, the happy couple's basement flooded, the carpet was ruined, the was trim destroyed. It was a mess.

Before we discuss what happened next, let's back up and put things in perspective. Maryland is an as-is state, meaning that, when you buy a house, it's all yours. Buyer beware. It's yours. Technically, my liability ends with a house closing. But my moral compass has its own rules—which is why I'll never become a millionaire doing this. I was determined to resolve this situation, especially after reviving a relic and watching the home find its perfect owners.

I started by talking the poor people off a ledge before going to look at the house myself. What was happening? It clearly wasn't a broken pipe. Water wasn't coming from the roof, and it certainly wasn't coming up under the ground. The house was solid as a rock—sitting on top of a hill.

Ground water was entering the house from unprecedented deluges of rain. I replayed every detail of the remodel in my mind, beginning at the top. When I replaced the roof during the remodel, I had added drains to avoid water ponding. In fact, before those changes were made, I had watched geese land in puddles on top of the house, treating the roof like their personal pond. Using careful calculations, I ran roof drains to the back of the house and out into the yard about 30 feet so they could empty where the hill sloped off. Painted to match the trim, these drains were both functional and architecturally pleasing.

After considering every other aspect of the project, I couldn't identify a specific water problem. So I asked the landscaper to double-check the grade. He re-graded, sodded, and tamped the soil down to make sure there was a good slope away from the house. Then I had the carpet removed and did damage control inside. The couple wanted to install new vinyl plank, so they bought the material and I installed it free of charge.

And it was good.

Until I received another text. Water was coming in again! After my concerted investment in this project, I was in disbelief that an issue I couldn't see had somehow materialized. I began to think more about the roof. Perhaps its performance changed when I installed the new material. During the remodel, we removed the tar and installed a rubber membrane that was much lighter. Now, apparently, the roof was allowing a lot of water to fall in one particular area—just above the basement stairway and window wells. But why? Had the roof become uneven over the years or was it something else? Either way, in heavy deluges, instead of running evenly off the roof, the water was now being funneled to one spot. And of course that one spot was the area that made the basement most vulnerable.

During this time, the couple took videos of heavy rains that looked like Niagara Falls coming over the roof near the basement access doors. The doors were watertight but the surrounding block and ground were porous. This time, the flooding was more contained so there was no need to pull out the floor. Still, the issue had to be resolved. I refocused my efforts on the top of the house. Typically, homes with flat roofs do not have gutters because their 3-foot overhang is designed to spread water evenly around the perimeter of the roof before dropping it several feet away from the foundation wall. Deciding that our heavy rains dictated a different technique, I added a black, heavy-duty gutter (matching the trim of house) with downspouts that tied into the existing roof drain system. Then, the landscaper added 18 inches of corrugated metal around the window wells before sealing them to the house and adding plexiglass covers. He removed the access doors and built up the walls with a full course of block before reinstalling them. Finally, he added dirt to ensure a visible slope away from the house before re-sodding the area.

And it was good.

After that, it continued to rain, day after day. My Facebook post said that I should be building arks instead of rehabbing houses.

And I received another text.

Although the basement access door itself was not leaking, water was now coming in under the door and the perimeter wall of the staircase leading into the basement. I was determined to solve this. While few rehabbers would invest as much heart, soul, and money in trying to make things right, my makeup doesn't allow me to leave people to fend for themselves. Thinking that the cover plates could become clogged if they were not large enough to handle the current rain levels, I bought bigger roof drain covers and deployed a team to install them.

This story exemplifies one of the hard realities you will face in the rehab business. Despite all your best efforts, you can't always make everything right. This situation was heartbreaking for me because it was heartbreaking for the homeowners. I couldn't control biblical rains and I couldn't change the way the original house had been built. But I could do everything within my power to mitigate the impact, and that's exactly what I did. I stood by my customers until we finally resolved the issue so they could get back to enjoying the home of their dreams.

Water. Not only does it cover nearly three-fourths of the earth, it relentlessly follows the law of gravity. That means there's a good chance some of it will eventually find its way into the basement. But now you know how to identify problems and divert water away from the house. You also know that surprises may happen despite all your best efforts to avoid them.

So, go ahead and build that man cave. Create a playroom the kids will love. Install a home theater. The sky's the limit. Because it's not a boat. It's a basement. And you can do so much more with a basement.

CHAPTER 22

There She Blows!

In school, they teach you that water runs downhill and that's basically all you need to know. Guess what? When it comes to plumbing, there's more to it than that.

Indoor plumbing has been around since the ancient Romans developed an aqueduct system of troughs that streamed water throughout a house. Like an open downspout, water was circulated to a kitchen or bathroom and back to its original outside source.

We've come a long way since then.

After Rome fell, plumbing systems evolved to a series of pipes that required pressure to move water upward as housing structures became larger and taller. With a piston that sucked water up from the well, a hand pump could be used to transfer water through pipes. Using a hand pump to service a whole house was ridiculous, resulting in several incarnations of pressurized systems that led to the development of the electric pump.

When you think about it, much of America—especially rural areas—didn't have electricity until the 1930s, minimizing public access to electric pump technology. During this time, steam pumps driven by turbine engines were used to generate pressure and move large quantities of water but they were expensive and difficult to maintain. This gave rise to the water tower that could serve a whole community from one large well run by a massive pump.

Water Towers

A water tower functions through the concept of gravity. As water is pumped higher into the holding tank, the greater the volume, the heavier the water pushes down through the pipes below. Assisted by gravity, water is moved throughout the plumbing system to serve houses as pressure is changed through a series of pipes that vary in size. At the water tower, the conduit may be a 10-inch steel main pipe with the capacity to carry vast quantities of water to the 6-inch pipes that feed specific streets. Those medium-sized pipes channel water into smaller pipes that enter a house to serve the ¾-inch interior plumbing. Throughout this feeder system, each time the pipe size is reduced, it decreases the pressure on the water coming out. If the plumbing is over-pressurized for the size of the pipe, it could cause a seam to rupture. For this reason, the pressure must be regulated, beginning with a gauge at the tower that monitors the constant force exerted to the water main.

In a public system, the municipality owns the tower and main line pipes, which are funded by taxes and/or water bills paid by the people they serve.

> **Mark-It: Each homeowner is individually responsible for the pipe that runs to the house from the supply line at the street and, of course, for the interior plumbing.**

It is important to understand this responsibility because the water supply line that feeds the house is especially susceptible to damage by homeowners who dig holes or plant trees in the wrong places. In older systems, an owner may encounter outdated cast iron pipes that rust, break down, and require replacement.

Pumping Stations

Another type of public pressurized system is a pumping station that uses a series of pumps to feed multiple areas instead of one central tower with a main line. Controlled by an electric, gas, or diesel pump, these systems efficiently serve large metropolitan areas. Surpassing the pressure and supply levels of multiple water towers, pumping stations draw water from a well, reservoir, or lake. After it is properly treated and filtered, the water is then sent through a series of pumps fed by multiple engines and backups. Unlike a water tower system that uses gravity and maintains a reserve in the holding tank, a pumping station is vulnerable to the same challenges you encounter at home: power failures, gas shortages, and more. In such instances, the system may shut down, stopping the water supply. Despite these issues, the pumping station is widely used in public areas.

Private Wells

Many homes are served by private wells, which are nothing more than holes in the ground at a depth where water is available and pumped up through straws of about 6 to 8 inches. In addition to functioning as a channel for the pipe that sucks water into the house, the straw provides a shaft for lowering the pump. Shaped like a bullet, the pump has a filter to remove sand, silt, and other debris. The pump clicks on when a pressure gauge in the house indicates that water is needed and shuts off when it is not. The round casing that protrudes into the yard is merely a housing for the pump's electric motor, so if it is accidentally hit, it won't spurt water like a fire hydrant.

When the pump is running, there is a constant change in pressure as the water comes on. For example, when you turn the shower on, the pressure gauge drops, the pump activates, and you get a burst of water. As long as the shower is on, the well runs according to the pressure setting at the pump. When you turn the faucet off, the pressure is changed and the pump deactivates.

Most modern wells are connected to a pressure tank by a pipe at the lowest level of the house. Typically blue, and 3 to 4 feet high, the tank has a bladder that works like a water balloon. When water is pumped into the tank, the bladder begins to stretch, lessening the pressure on the pump. As the tank fills, water pushes against the bottom and sides, stretching the bladder to about one-third the size of the cylinder. Water continues to expand the bladder inside the cylinder until it cannot increase anymore, sending a signal to turn off the pump at the bottom of the well.

From the pressure tank, a pipe channels water flow based on the size of the opening. In this way, regulating the water pressure in your house is much like controlling the pressure in a water balloon by holding your finger over the hole. The size of the opening determines the amount of pressure, creating a controlled leak that allows water into your house.

Two pressure gauges are used to regulate the process. One alerts the pump when the bladder is losing pressure, tripping it on to refill. A second gauge tells the tank how to maintain pressure in the house. Usually located at the top of the tank, this valve functions as a spigot to adjust pressure in the plumbing, making it more feasible for houses with wells to have good water flow.

Managing Pressure

Regardless of the water source, constant pressure is integral to a functional plumbing system. Variances in pressure within the house can cause a multitude of problems with appliances and other equipment.

> **Mark-It**: Typically, water pressure in your plumbing should be set around 30-35 per square inch (psi).

Given this substantial weight on the pipes, it is important to have plumbing that is rated for pressurized systems. If the wrong pipes are used for 35 psi, they could actually blow apart. That is why all plumbing is now stamped for its weight rating; staying at the low end of that spectrum should help to avoid damage to the system. When the system is over-pressurized, the first signs of damage will be at the joints, elbows, and seams.

Temperature fluctuations can impact water flow throughout the house. Think about the ice cube trays that were used before automatic dispensers became popular. We learned to fill the trays halfway, knowing the water would expand as it froze. In the same way, the volume of water in your pipes increases as the water molecules cool and swell. When water is pumped into cool pipes in the basement and not used for a while, it may linger in the pipe and get chilly, altering the volume of water in the pipe. With nowhere for the water to go, the plumbing pipes may become over-pressurized. To deal with this, many new systems feature small, floating relief tanks that draw water in to help manage the impact of heating and cooling changes. Uncommon as recently as five years ago, these relief tanks are now mandatory in most jurisdictions. Even with a pressurization tank, if pipes extend through a cool, unfinished basement to heated, finished main floors, there may be fluctuations in pressure when the water is turned on. Along with these issues, temperature changes from summer to winter can wreak havoc on a system.

> **Mark-It**: As rehabbers, contractors, and homeowners, we are always looking for ways to maintain constant pressure in the house.

One solution is to install pressurized pipes in basements, outside walls, and unfinished areas, and this is often required by code. Through varying seasons, municipalities constantly monitor and adjust the water pressure at the system level, and the same should be done within the home. The meter for a public system also measures water usage to determine the bill. These meters formerly functioned like the odometer in a car, spinning to record the gallons of water used in the home. With new technology, current meters have an LED beam that registers usage electronically, making on-site visits from utility companies unnecessary.

Types of Plumbing

Now that we've discussed the overall system, let's focus on the components. There are many types of piping, beginning with early versions made of cast iron and steel. These products may become compromised over time and should be replaced. After years of use, the metal will break down near a seam, causing rust to form, leaching unhealthy chemicals such as lead or magnesium into the water flow. For this reason, it is important to conduct a test—especially in older homes—to reveal what is in the water. Does this mean you shouldn't buy a house that has old plumbing? Obviously not, and there are different ways to approach the issue. Since it is an expensive proposition to change all the plumbing in a house, some homeowners prefer to maintain an older system knowing that they will not use the water for drinking. Water that may be fine for taking a shower or running through the toilet may require filters for human consumption. The best solution, if financially feasible, is to modernize the plumbing.

Copper

In an effort to improve on primitive systems, copper emerged as a popular solution that does not rust or break down over time. While copper may patina or have a light reaction, it doesn't leach dangerous chemicals into the water flow. In fact, copper has several benefits, making it a safe and repairable choice.

Polyvinyl Chloride (PVC)

As demand increased over time, copper became scarcer and more expensive, creating a shift to polyvinyl chloride (PVC) pipes. After undergoing many incarnations to address product stability and health issues, PVC is popular in homes today, with specified ratings for pressurized use.

If you are rehabbing or purchasing a home with PVC pipes, there are a few things you need to know about the product's evolution. Older versions of PVC will become brittle over time, especially when exposed to extreme temperature fluctuations. In addition, the original glue used to seal PVC joints and fittings was short-lived and poor-performing, creating more failures. You will see evidence of these issues in moldy, wet houses where PVC pipes have splintered, shattered, or exploded under pressure.

Polybutylene Plastic

Attempts to rectify these problems led to some new fiascos. One, in particular, was an attempt to replace PVC with polybutylene plastic. Replicating a sturdier version of a garden hose, this product was a small, flexible pipe that gained popularity in the mid-1980s. Before poly butylene was available, plumbing sections had to be cut to length and joined together at every turn. With multiple joints, each one created the opportunity for failure. Poly butylene was going to save everyone from the time, extra product, and headaches by allowing a plumber to install pipes like an electrician running wires. With the new "wonder product," multiple feeds could be routed through holes from the main junction all the way to a second- or third-floor bathroom. The smooth material was easily manipulated through holes and around turns, seamlessly traversing the route from the water's point of origin to the sink where it was needed. With no joints or connections, these flexible pipes could travel from one end of the house to another without connections. Easy-peasy.

Sounds great, right? That's what everyone thought back when I was studying architecture in the 1980s. This was going to be the plumbing product of the future. As it turned out, there were two big issues with poly butylene. First, it tended to catch, rip, and rupture when it was pulled through holes, routed around obstacles, or punctured by a stray nail—and repairs were complicated. A special tape with water-soluble glue had to be applied in a time-consuming system of depressurizing and drying. Unfortunately, poly butylene's flexibility exerted more stress on the repair joints, making them unreliable and subject to long-term problems.

The other issue with poly butylene plastic was far more devastating and it took years to discover. The product is made from an oil-based chemical that is poisonous when consumed. This happened in many areas where it leached into the water. As a result, the installation of poly butylene plumbing is illegal in most municipalities and must be removed where it exists.

Modern PVC

Although plastic in plumbing has traversed a rocky road, PVC has gradually become the mainstay in new construction. The fewest changes have occurred with plastic applications in drain systems where pressure on the pipes is minimal and health issues are not a concern. A lighter version of PVC has become a popular source for roof vents and wastewater drains in many houses that use copper for supply lines.

These changes bring us to where we are today. Current supply lines are typically made of a high-pressure PVC pipe that is thicker than the earlier versions while still easy to cut and join.

Mark-It: For tracking purposes and to easily confirm that the right product is in use, today's PVC piping is cream-colored (rather than bright white), marked with a yellow line, dated, and stamped with manufacturing locations and details.

In addition, a special yellow or purple glue is applied to the pipes. This glue is projected to have a longer lifespan than the piping itself—perhaps 30 to 50 years—and over time we'll learn if that's true. As a rehabber, be sure your plumbing lines and drain systems have the proper dating, stamping, and other safety features. If not, expect an inspector to call you out.

Hot and Cold

Your plumbing system's supply is split when water enters the house, with one line going to a water heater.

Mark-It: As my plumber reminds me a thousand times each week, it is not called a *hot* water heater, because there would be no need to heat water that is already hot. Call it a water heater and sound like a pro.

The other line feeds the cold supply, and the two are not mixed until they arrive at a   connection point. In most cases, this would be a diverter that combines hot and cold water at a fixture such as a single-handled faucet at a shower or sink. Enabled by the diverter, the handle is rotated to determine the right mix of hot and cold water, or to send water in multiple directions in a tub faucet or overhead sprinkler. With separate faucets for hot and cold water, older systems did not use diverters. In these versions, still available today, water is manually mixed by the amount sent into the pipes from each side before it flows from the spout.

Metal plumbing is especially susceptible to expansion and contraction. When hot water is run through the pipe from the water heater, it expands as the heated liquid travels through it and contracts when it changes to cold. This explains why we have separate hot and cold water lines until they reach a diverter. Otherwise, we'd be asking for trouble, by exerting a risky temperature differential on metal piping. While PVC pipes are not as susceptible to these temperature changes, they are fragile and can easily shatter in freezing situations.

Drains

Like rain on a leaky roof, water is always looking for a way out, and that brings us to drain systems.

> **Mark-It**: When evaluating the drains in a rehab, make sure all plumbing pieces are water tight at the bottom of each sink or tub.

Toilets are a specific type of drain system affixed with a wax ring that is bolted on the flange and pressed into the floor—without glue—at the time of installation. When the water drains with no pressure on the joint, the toilet functions properly.

Remember that the water flowing into a drain is not pressurized. A drinking straw provides a good analogy for understanding this concept. If you hold your finger over a straw and dip it into a drink, the liquid will remain in the tube. This happens because the water must be displaced by air in order to drain. In this example, the straw acts as a plumbing pipe and the hole at the top functions as the drain that opens in order to release water. If you were to seal the top of a sink drain, you could stop the water flow below due to a lack of air.

For this reason, plumbing must be vented at multiple points, depending on the size and configuration of a house. While every drain requires a vent stack, they can be combined, alleviating the need for one at every sink and fixture. Often made of PVC, this stack extends straight up through the roof and is visible on the outside of a house. If the project is done by Harry Homeowner, you might see these stacks on the front of a house, but good builders work to place them inconspicuously at the back. In a condominium or apartment building, the vents are combined into one major stack, serving the important function of preventing airlock and allowing the system to drain properly. Over time, vent stacks may become clogged by a bird's nest or a buildup of leaves, causing them to hold water, increase in weight, and exert pressure on the system. Since a drain system is not built for pressure, this force can easily lead to leaks or plumbing backups.

Mark-It: In each project you encounter, take time to check the vents, remove clogs, and ensure that the drain system is functioning properly.

P Traps

The P trap is designed to handle clogs that may occur beyond a toilet bowl or other fixture. I'm not sure why this is called a P trap because it looks more like an S; we'll let the English majors sort that out. Located under the drain, the P trap is a curved pipe that has one job—to hold water. Here's how it works. As drain waste flows into sewer lines or septic systems, gases and smells can build up and work their way back into your house. Thankfully, the P trap uses a water barrier to prevent backflow, creating a permanent seal for every sink, tub, or toilet. On a toilet, the P trap is built into the fixture itself, with the bowl acting as the top half of the trap and the remainder below, evidenced by the S shape on the side of the toilet. In bathtubs and shower drains, P traps are usually set in the floor under the fixture. Since P traps can also hold hair and sediment, they occasionally clog but are easily cleared with a sink plunger. These tools are small, flat versions of the standard plungers used for toilets.

Assessing Plumbing in Home Rehabs

As you consider new projects, it is important to identify plumbing issues early in the process because they can significantly impact your budget and permitting timeline. Here's a recap of the types of plumbing lines you can expect to see in older homes.

1) *Copper supply lines and drain systems:* This version was common when copper was the plentiful metal of choice. As long as the materials are in good condition, this type of system is good to go.

2) *Copper supply lines with PVC drain systems:* As copper became less available and more expensive, it was common to use it only for the lines supplying the house, while incorporating more affordable PVC in other areas such as drains. If the system is in good condition, this configuration is perfectly acceptable.

3) *PVC for both supply lines and drain systems:* As long as all piping is rated and stamped for safe use and in good condition, this system is fine. In homes built before the stamping system was in place, check for brittle pipes and be advised that the product may not pass inspection depending on the type of plastic used.

4) *Copper supply lines with steel or cast-iron drain systems:* While there is no health risk in having a cast iron or steel drain line that will not be used as a water supply, these products are likely to rust over time. There is nothing worse than a leaking sewer line, so I recommend replacing these old-style pipes. If the drains are in excellent condition and your budget does not allow for replacement, a spray/primer product such as Rust-Oleum may help to control exterior rust, although it will not stop the pipes from rusting inside and causing future leaks.

5) *Cast iron or steel supply lines and drain systems:* Since these supply lines could be leaching dangerous particles into the water supply, they must be replaced or fitted with a proper filtering system. Likewise, it makes sense to replace the drains, since they will be susceptible to rust and leaks.

6) *Combination of copper and PVC supply lines and PVC drains:* As long as the PVC is properly rated, the system is in good condition, and the components are connected with special couplings designed for these two products, this type of system is perfectly acceptable. Unlike the issue with mixing aluminum and copper in electrical systems, there is no problem with connecting PVC and copper plumbing. In fact, due to the cost of copper, this combination has become quite common.

7) *Polybutylene supply lines:* Given the significant health concerns, it would be immoral and irresponsible to leave this product in the house. Replace it.

Now that you understand how water enters the house and travels through and out of it, I'll share tips to help you avoid plumbing pitfalls.

If you're not familiar with a product or subject, don't pretend to understand. Arm yourself with knowledge and know what to look for when you start each new project. Whether you're a rehabber or the purchaser of a rescued house, your budget is real—not fake—and failing to set aside adequate money to deal with an issue can lead to a financial disaster. Talk to experts, read a book, and search the Internet to learn what you need to know before you move forward.

As a rehabber, be upfront and honest with your buyers about decisions, products, and techniques. If you're the purchaser, talk to the rehabber and ask questions.

> **Mark-It: Rather than hiding things from you, a good rehabber will collaborate with you to make smart, project-specific decisions.**

Confront decisions with common sense and alleviate fear. Every situation is unique. The rehabber may prefer to spend money on granite in the kitchen rather than replacing cast iron drain pipes that are in good shape and functioning properly. In that case, a choice may be made to forego the inspection. This approach is fine as long as the rehabber provides full disclosure, setting clear expectations that the buyer may need to make a replacement at a later date if leaks arise.

Understand your project from a home inspector's perspective. Know what to look for and stay ahead of the game.

Just because something is old, it doesn't mean it is inferior. While standards change, if an old product works and does not endanger anyone, there's no need to replace it, although an adaptation may improve its functionality. With every decision you make along the way, it is important to be upfront about the issues, make ethical choices, and give thought to the outcome. Never take shortcuts that could be deemed dangerous or put a future buyer at risk.

* * * *

In terms of plumbing, the most impactful stories happened early in my career, before I learned to avoid certain problems. Knowledge is power when it comes to overcoming mistakes and suffice it to say that I've acquired a lot of power through the years. Some of my knowledge comes from mistakes that are so unforgettable I'd never make them again. For example—it's worth repeating—don't open the refrigerator in a vacant house that hasn't had electrical power in five years. No kidding, it smells so bad you can actually feel it through your skin. Learning this alone is worth the price of buying this book.

Testing Day Beats Demo Day

On HGTV, the most exciting moment seems to be Demo Day, when everybody and his brother takes a hammer to the house. For me, the most exciting day is Testing Day when I turn on the utilities and find out how the mechanicals are truly functioning—or not. While plumbing issues are fairly easy to fix when discovered early on, they are a pain in the neck to find later. So, I'm always anxious to turn on the water and keep my fingers crossed.

Plumbing, in particular, has a funny way of communicating its issues in a vacant house where the pressure has built up in faucets that have been closed and sealed. When a system is restarted and water is pumped through empty pipes, air is released through cracks and loose joints, making the most interesting whistling and moaning sounds. As the plumbing shrieks to life, every noise helps me identify leaks.

On Testing Day, I start in the basement or some other low point where water enters the house. Step one is to turn on the well pump to see if water is available. After making sure every fixture in the house is turned off, I open the valve in the basement to release water into the plumbing. This is when I listen. I strain to hear moaning, whistling, and other sounds that indicate leaks and telltale issues. Or, best of all, I hear the sweet silence of a problem-free system.

This is the story of a house that I encountered early in my career. Vacant for many years, the residence was served by a well. On Testing Day I was alone. That was mistake #1 and it was big. You're about to learn why I will never again go into Testing Day without a wingman.

After ensuring that all the faucets were turned off, I went to the basement of the three-story home, turned on the water, and listened for the sounds of cracked pipes. This house had the older style of PVC which meant there were some brittle splits. They weren't just joint issues, but splits in several places that ran parallel along the pipes. These types of splits howl the most so I heard a lot of whistling but no evidence of gushing water in the basement. I was excited, knowing that water was flowing through the pipes with just a small drip near the staircase. Hearing nothing else, my confidence grew, thinking this was going to be good.

As you might imagine, it is difficult to troubleshoot a multi-level water system from a basement-only perspective. It stands to reason that, the farther I might walk from the valve in the basement, the longer it would take me to turn the water off if I happened to encounter a problem. On this particular day, that thought hadn't crossed my mind.

I left my post at the valve in the basement and went to the first floor to check the kitchen. After seeing that all was well, I scaled the steps to the second floor. I could still hear the sounds of water in the pipes signaling that pressurized water was moving along and exiting, although I didn't know where. Two flights from the valve in the basement, I stuck my head in the shower of the first bathroom and found nothing. The bathtub, too, was free of water.

At that point, I was thinking this was crazy because I could hear water running. The pump had not shut off, so water was definitely being pushed through the pipes. I checked the private bath in the master bedroom. One side of the tub had a hand shower with a flexible pipe you could pick up—like the French people do—to sit in the shower and hose yourself off. I never understood why the French shower this way instead of using a fixed shower and curtain but I guess that's pretty standard over there. For us, not so much. Anyway, this flexible shower thingy was sitting in the bottom of the tub. Then I realized it wasn't sitting at all—it was dancing, with water shooting out. The flexible tube had dry rotted and broken off, causing water to run into the bathtub and down the drain. That was good news, right? Water was running into the tub and down the drain causing no additional damage other than the one small drip I noticed in the basement.

Here's where my really stupid mistake comes in. Obviously, water was exiting the pipe to the hand shower thingy because the water was turned on at the tub even though I thought it was off. Apparently, to turn off the handheld shower you had to move the diverter at the faucet in the other direction while also adjusting the hot and cold knobs. I turned the diverter *to shut off the water to the hand shower and, for about 15 seconds, the system quieted down. But I still heard water running. That meant all the plastic plumbing pipes throughout the house were getting pressurized due to this change at the top of the house. By shutting off the diverter at the highest level, the plastic pipes were pressurized all the way down to the pump that continued pushing until it hit the setting of about 27 to 32 psi. As the force continued, I stood in the upstairs bathroom thinking I'd resolved the problem by turning the diverter off.*

Then I heard God-awful pops, cracks, and screaming sounds. I was in the house by myself, freaking out, and thinking, "what the heck?" I left the master bathroom just as one of those menacing sounds launched a portion of the PVC pipe at the shut-off valve from under the vanity. As the knob flew to the other side of the bathroom, water poured into the room. Since the shut-off valve had just been destroyed, I ran toward the basement, only to be met by water entering the hallway from the other bathroom. With the carpet recently removed, water flowed onto the plywood like a gusher and was running down the stairs in a waterfall. When I reached the bottom of the stairs, I saw water shooting straight up from a faucet in the kitchen where the handle had blown off. It was firing directly into a light fixture above the sink before running back down the counter and onto the tile floor.

Running around the corner on the main floor, I passed another bathroom with water seeping under the door frame. On my way to the valve in the far corner of the basement, I felt like I was in a water park, trying—but not succeeding—to dodge deluges from multiple locations. By the time I reached the valve and turned it off, I was soaking wet.

This whole fiasco could have been avoided if I had someone—like my friend Mario, for example—with me in the house on Testing Day. On my own, I made quite a mess of things. Even though I couldn't change the core issues, having people assist with the plumbing test would have minimized the ensuing damage from a system that had been extremely compromised. While I manned the valve in the basement, I could have stationed people on the first and second floors to check the system.

Through years of neglect, the pipes in this house became dry rotted and brittle. Sudden pressurization led to the complete breakdown of all the plumbing. After I hired a plumber to fix the four or five broken pipes, turning the water back on revealed even more breaks in a system filled with weak links. It soon became evident that we needed to replace the entire plumbing system. Fortunately, I had included the relocation of two bathrooms and full rehabs of the others in my budget, so there was a sufficient amount to cover most of the cost. This—along with the 10% contingency I always include in my overall number—saved the day.

This experience was another lesson learned. While you can't anticipate every issue that will arise on a project, you can always fix or replace things as long as you're prepared. Create a budget cushion that makes the landing easier when you have to take a fall. Because falls will happen, and sometimes they're waterfalls.

CHAPTER 23

Don't Be Like Cousin Eddie

We all remember the scene from *National Lampoon's Christmas Vacation*—my favorite movie—when Cousin Eddie empties the septic waste from his RV into the storm drain at the street. While the neighbors' reactions make for a funny moment in an already hilarious movie, septic systems are often the least amusing and most expensive part of a rehabber's world. A responsible rehabber will disclose septic issues and provide new owners with a working system that has a reasonable life span. This accountability differentiates a reputable business from a flipper who may ignore major issues and pass them along to an unsuspecting buyer.

Outpacing the Outhouse

Let's talk about where wastewater goes when you flush it away. Before indoor plumbing, this was quite simple. With a pump at the kitchen sink, people could fill a bowl, wash up, and dump the contents outside. With an outhouse serving as the family bathroom, I can't imagine anything more unpleasant on a cold, snowy night than running outside to get relief. Interestingly, the outhouse is an early version of today's septic pits and drain fields. Just like an outhouse, these systems transfer waste until it is absorbed into the ground. Modern portable toilets add chemicals to break down the waste and control the odor with a tank in the bottom that can be pumped out regularly.

As plumbing developed and moved inside, drains from sinks, showers, tubs, toilets, and washing machines were fed into a master drain at the lowest point in the house. There, all the waste was collected and channeled out through a single pipe. If you have public utilities, the sewage runs through a system that is similar to the reverse of the plumbing water source. The sewage leaves your house in a pipe that continues to grow in diameter until it reaches the treatment facility where solids are separated. The water is then filtered and treated before being channeled into a river or stream. Separated solids and trash can be made into useful products such as fertilizer or may be burned off as odorous, methane gas. If you live near a treatment plant you know what I'm talking about.

The Ins and Outs of Septic Systems

Those without public services must deal with at-home waste disposal systems that are regulated by an unfathomable number of codes. Septic systems typically require a homesite with at least one-quarter acre of land and they are prevalent in rural areas that are beyond reach of public services. Since I'm not an expert on septic systems, I'll give you the Reader's Digest version.

Counties, municipalities, and environmental agencies dictate the type and location of septic systems on drawings that must be approved prior to installation. There is no way around stringent requirements such as these:

1) A treatment system cannot be placed anywhere near a well, whether the well is on site or on a neighboring lot.

2) The location must be designed to ensure that the septic system will not contaminate a natural resource such as an active stream or creek.

3) The soils in the ground should be sufficient to absorb the liquid waste in a reasonable amount of time—even during rainy seasons—so sewage does not emerge at the ground's surface. An analysis of soil types and absorption rates are key to ensuring acceptable conditions for a septic system.

There are many types and configurations of septic systems. Some are developed as mounded structures that pump wastewater uphill. Appearing as a berm of dirt in the yard, these systems may require a big chunk of change, depending on the complexity. Even though septic issues are usually repairable, I tend to avoid these types of properties, if possible, because many buyers do not understand them. In addition to impacting your profit, a single situation can sink your business.

> **Mark-It**: Before purchasing a property with a septic system, I always get an inspection from a qualified professional who will check the tank, test the drain fields, and ensure that the system is good for at least five to ten years.

How Percs Work

If you buy a home on an acre or more of land, there is a good chance that it will contain multiple percs, or approved locations, conducive to a septic field. The process to determine these percs is actually quite primitive, much like using a dipstick to measure a car engine's oil level:

- A perc tester uses tools that include a wooden spike with nails affixed at different heights, a bucket of water, and a stopwatch.
- Water is poured into a hole to determine the amount of time it takes to absorb into the soil.
- The tester twists the wooden spike into the ground and pours in about five gallons of water.
- The results are recorded in a test rate, which is the time it takes the liquid to reach specific intervals on the spike.

With the perc test, the jurisdiction specifies an allowable absorption rate to approve a perc hole. If one hole is dug and doesn't perc, another attempt will be made within 10 to 20 feet, depending on the code. Completed perc locations are marked as failed or passed on a map for the benefit of future buyers. Perc inspection rates and regulations vary by jurisdiction. In some cases, two approved percs are required to build or replace a system. The reason for this is that a drain field may eventually fail, necessitating a new installation.

> **Mark-It**: **Percs are usually valid for a specified length of time, so familiarize yourself with costs and codes that apply in your area.**

As you can see, perc tests are relatively inexpensive but the costs can add up. And, with no limit on the number of holes that can be dug, some properties quickly turn into Swiss cheese. That reminds me of a story.

A while back, I purchased a house to rehab in an exclusive, country club-style neighborhood built in the 1960s. In addition to the rehab property, the deal included an adjacent lot that the original owner had purchased to insulate himself from his neighbors. It's amazing the lengths to which people will go in order to avoid human contact. Properties in the neighborhood exceeded an acre, so homeowners already had to go on a hike to borrow a cup of sugar.

The county had long ago made public water and sewer available to this neighborhood, but the original residents didn't want to tear up their pristine streets and yards for the mere convenience of reliable toilet flushes. Many years later, this lack of foresight resulted in a community of failing septic systems and expensive remedies that threatened the homes' future livability and overall value.

Since the lots I was buying conveyed together, I planned to subdivide them to expand my opportunity. During the purchase, I received notice that the side lot did not perc, although I could see that the county was clearly taxing it as if it were buildable. Always looking for an opportunity—and rarely taking no for an answer—I decided to pursue the perc issue to determine if I had a viable, buildable lot on my hands. I started by fighting the battle to schedule a perc test, which involved a lot of begging and assembling of random crap. The main argument in my favor was that, for decades, the county had been assessing the property at a rate commensurate with buildable lots. I reasoned that if the lot were not buildable then it had been over-assessed for years, entitling me (as the property owner) to a significant refund. That argument provided the leverage I needed to get the perc test scheduled.

The perc team arrived and dug three holes. One passed and two failed, which was a big deal because someone somewhere determined that you need not one, but two, passing perc holes within a specified radius of each other. By the way, county officials ruling on perc tests are about as clear as NFL referees trying to officiate a game these days. They talk in circles, assess the same situation differently on different days, and sometimes reverse their calls.

Giving this some thought and looking at the huge lot in front of me, I wondered how I could have only one good perc. After all, there was over an acre to work with and no well to navigate around because a public water line had ultimately made it to the community. When I requested an additional perc, the on-site team explained that they needed special equipment to address a shelf of rock they had encountered. After I paid them to come back with new equipment, they dug three more holes and again one passed.

Now I had six holes on the property and—hooray—two of them were good.

As it turned out, the two good holes were not near each other. One was at the back right of the lot, while the other was positioned at the front left. The septic could go in either location and, obviously, I preferred the back right. Here's where NFL-style regulations again came into play. Another perc rule states that you must be able to draw a straight line from one good perc to the other—without crossing a failed perc. You can't make this stuff up. It's like roughing the passer these days. You can tackle the quarterback as long as you don't touch him above or below the waist.

So, I continued to fight back.

After multiple trips and tests, I had about $5,000 invested in the Swiss-cheese-perc project but I was willing to keep going because I had a new idea. Since I owned the adjoining lot where I was conducting the rehab, I could move the lot lines. The existing house already had a new septic system, so I would do more perc tests on that property to align with the hole that had passed on the front left of the adjacent lot. If I could get a new hole approved and draw a straight line between the two holes, I could re-subdivide and have a successful perc situation. When I proposed this to the county, you would have thought I was asking for someone to ship me $3 million in an offshore bank account. I'm not sure why this was so complicated, but they finally couldn't come up with a logical reason to deny it, so I finally got them to agree.

Then, just like the NFL, upon further review the county officials cited an existing, obscure rule. Now they also wanted me to find a repair field for the brand-new septic system on property that had already qualified for a 20- to 30-year perc. There was no arguing. They made a ruling and I had to comply.

The perc team dug more holes, this time on the lot where the house was located. Three holes were burrowed near the successful perc on the adjacent lot, and all three were good, fast percs. Finally, I was in the clear. I could draw straight lines between percs and move the lot lines to accommodate my plan. It was so perfect.

As you know, the NFL is always changing the rules and the same is true of the county. There is a relatively recent regulation that says you can have a paved driveway over a portion—but not all—of a septic field. And, of course, I had a driveway between the two perc holes and, of course, it covered more of the septic field than allowed. So I had to move the driveway to get the perc to qualify.

At this point, I had spent about $8,000 to create nine perc holes. Although moving the driveway would cost another $8,000 to $10,000, I decided it was a worthwhile investment since my agent had assured me I could sell the lot for $150,000. At the time, it seemed like a no-brainer so I dug up the driveway and moved it. With the driveway relocated and the lot lines adjusted via a give-and-take land swap, I installed the septic system, complete with a pump to deal with a hill that, of course, landed in the middle of it all. Then I installed a sign to sell the lot.

After rehabbing and selling the house on the main property, the adjacent lot is still on the market (at the reduced rate of $135,000, if you're interested) and it's testing my patience because it shouldn't have been this hard. Even though the trenches for the drain fields are the same size and *length as those for the large rancher on the main property, the county would only approve the adjacent lot for a two-bedroom house, based on the perc. Keep in mind that this is a neighborhood filled with massive, four- and five-bedroom structures. Potential builders for this lot are skittish about marketing a two-bedroom house in a neighborhood where people want one-level living with multiple bedrooms. To see any profit on this whole crazy experience, I will likely build on the property myself.*

And then I'll go watch some football.

Why the Grass is Greener Over There

Now that we have identified septic field locations, let's talk about how they work. When you flush a toilet, the liquid and solid waste are combined and carried out of the house through a pipe that exits at the lowest point. Unless there is an ejector pump involved, the waste flows downhill into a septic tank. Comprised of block or poured concrete and often set into the ground, these receptacles are topped by lids made of steel, wood, or concrete. Over time, steel lids rust and wooden ones rot away, leading to today's versions in concrete or Acrylonitrile Butadiene Styrene (ABS) plastic.

Smaller than you might imagine, the septic tank size is determined by the number of people who will live in the house. Municipalities calculate the housing capacity by specifying a bedroom allowance based on the property's drain field space and absorption rate. Interestingly, municipalities don't specify the number of bathrooms a home may have—only the bedrooms—due to a theory that one bedroom equals two people. This means there could be a three-bedroom, two-bathroom house or a three-bedroom, six-bathroom house and it wouldn't matter as long as the system was approved for three bedrooms.

The bottom line is that people don't always play by these rules. They will pull perc tests for an approved three-bedroom house and build a version that disguises the fourth bedroom as an office. This becomes a problem when someone with a gaggle of kids later purchases the house, putting two children in each of the perceived four bedrooms. After eight years or so, this family is likely to have a septic issue.

Mark-It: Pay special attention to percs and notice how Harry Homeowner might have impacted the septic system over time by adding bedrooms in the basement.

Once the wastewater and solids reach the septic tank, they are separated, with the heavier solids falling to the bottom and the liquid rising to the top. To ensure that solid waste does not find its way to the septic field, the pipe that exits the tank is higher than the one that brings the waste in, and a baffle is often included as an additional barrier. While the pipe positioning is important for most tanks to work properly, they may be located at the same height when a baffle is in place. Consider the watertight sections of the *Titanic*. As water came in, it filled the first chamber before overflowing into the next and working its way through. In a similar septic tank scenario, most of the solid waste is caught in the first chamber and, when that overflows, only liquid moves into subsequent sections. In many tanks, there are three chambers, making it highly unlikely for solids to find their way through. As a result of these methods, the organic solids never leave the tank but eventually break down. It is only the water from showers, sinks, toilets, dishwashers, and washers that flows over the solids and ends up in the drain field.

The pipe leading from the septic tank to the drain field branches off into three fingers of primary, secondary, and tertiary trenches. While each system works the same regardless of its size, the length and depth of these trenches is determined when the system is designed and approved by the county. Wastewater flows out of the tank, through a pipe, and into the drain field channeled by the first trench or perforated pipe. With dimensions determined by the soil's absorption rate, this trench or pipe will be filled with gravel, providing ample opportunity for liquid to be absorbed from the sides and bottom. If this first trench becomes saturated on a rainy day, the liquid flows into the second trench and then on to the third in the rare cases when it is needed.

Mark-It: It is important to refrain from planting trees or digging holes in a drain field because it would ruin the trench. Yet, it may be okay to add a walkway or pavers over the field since it functions through absorption—not evaporation.

If the drain field becomes overly saturated and the highly-fertilized waste water rises, it could make the ground above soft. Even if it is not wet enough to soften the ground, the nitrates may make the grass greener, which is how we got the joke about the grass always being greener over the drain field. Of course, you don't regulate what occurs in a drain field; it happens naturally. All this activity is going on underground in your yard while kids are playing on the swing set above, and you never think about it unless there is a problem.

Like many other property features, drain fields have evolved over time. They used to be large seepage pits, about 8 to 10 feet in diameter, dug deep into the ground and lined with brick or block to keep the walls from collapsing. The joints between the blocks were not filled in, so the liquids seeped through the spaces while the solids were trapped inside. Filling from the bottom, they eliminated the need for a tank. Yet, due to their extreme depth, seepage pits were almost impossible to pump. With an absorption area limited to the circumference of the pit, their capabilities were inferior to a standard drain field.

In some regions where a house has already been built and there is no place to install a drain field, the only repair is to bury a cylindrical holding tank in the ground. Since these systems have to be pumped on a regular basis, you need to follow a maintenance schedule and provide truck access.

> **Mark-It**: Holding tank systems are not cheap, and lenders will require buyers to add this amount to qualify for a mortgage. I find it impossible to sell a house with holding tanks so I don't do it. It's not worth the aggravation.

CHAPTER 24

This Could Be Shocking

Unlike plumbing, most people understand the history of electricity so I won't go into the life of Thomas Edison. Yet, there are some important electrical issues that will impact your decisions as a buyer or rehabber. Read on.

It All Starts Somewhere...

While plumbing diverts liquid that already exists; electricity requires the creation of something that doesn't. Regardless of how it is generated, there's no doubt that electricity will be part of our future. As a nation, we continue to develop greater efficiency and savings through the use of oil, natural gas, and propane. It seems that we are on track to use these non-renewable fossil fuels until they are depleted. Politics aside, any realistic human being has to agree that fossil fuels may not be the best way to maximize our future. Thank God there are people out there who are always researching alternatives.

Since it's manmade, electricity can be generated in a variety of ways, from solar to wind, water turbine, nuclear, and more. With proper monitoring and control, I believe nuclear power is going to be the long-term solution, accompanied by solar, wind, and water backups.

Although current costs are difficult to wrap our heads around, an all-electric home is likely to be the wave of the future. Yet, there are issues. Like water pressure, the problem with electricity is that its effectiveness declines as it extends farther from the source. Electricity generated from a dam may traverse three states, sacrificing power each time it goes through a substation. Unless multiple hubs are added, power for the end user may drop to an inadequate level.

For other sources such as solar, wind, and water, availability and cost come into play, forcing area homeowners to rely on gas or oil. Currently, I'm not a fan of solar because I believe the industry is product-based rather than consumer-driven. Motivating homeowners with the promise of a power bill discount, solar companies slap panels on scores of homes. While not owned by the consumer, these panels can ruin the roof, look unsightly, and detract from the home's overall value. Solar shingles, now in development, could solve some of these issues by providing a roofing alternative that absorbs power from the sun. When perfected, this product is likely to increase the value of a home and provide another step toward our all-electric society.

> **Mark-It: When developing project strategies for rehabs, I help people think long term.**

If money were no issue, I'd install geothermal in every home, but most buyers are unwilling to cover that cost in a renovated house. Otherwise, I'm a heat pump guy all the way. I often encourage buyers to consider an all-electric house with a backup gas or oil furnace.

... and Then it Goes Somewhere

Once generated, electricity is transported to your home from a substation through a local transmission box or pole. Regardless of how the lines are configured, power is stepped down at several junctures before it reaches a house. This system hasn't changed much over the years except that electricity previously carried on overhead poles is often now buried underground. By minimizing the impact from tree growth and severe weather, the move to underground lines has reduced long-term maintenance issues.

A Look Inside the Panel Box

After power reaches the house, it is routed to a panel box where it is broken down and distributed through the structure via wires or circuits. Standard amperages for homes vary with the age of a structure. An older house may have 100-amp service that is sufficient for most needs, especially if efficient LED lights are used. However, the addition of power-hungry appliances such as microwaves, hair dryers, and space heaters are driving demand for higher amp services. As a result, an older home may be underpowered for modern needs.

Today, the standard voltage in a residential home is 110, along with 220 for ranges, electric dryers, and appliances that draw more power. In a modern panel box, the voltages are easily identified (and should be marked on the panel door), because 220 appears as a double wide breaker while 110 is single. If the panel box is small and all the breakers are full, chances are it is undersized and will need to be upgraded. Depending on the jurisdiction, such changes may be required by code.

> **Mark-It**: **In assessing a house for rehab, look for a panel box with sufficient expansion space to accommodate future needs.**

Flexible by design, the panel box got its name because it provides multiple ways for an electrician to connect wiring through changes in technology and home improvement. Some homes have old-style circuit boxes with a series of primitive fuses that look like shotgun shells stuck between metal brackets. In these boxes, a switch is flipped to turn the power on or off. With all the wiring exposed, these outdated circuit breaker systems are especially dangerous, increasing the likelihood of electrocution or fire. Another type of old-school box had screw-in fuses that could be twisted into sockets like light bulbs. Popular in the 1950s, people tried creative but crazy troubleshooting methods such as shoving paper clips inside the box. With no chance of passing inspection, if you encounter these types of panel boxes, they will have to go.

Fuses in older panel boxes were usually glass, with a thin filament inside that was less resistant than the wire running into the wall. If too many things were plugged into one outlet, causing an excessive draw on the wiring, the fuse provided a safeguard to alert the homeowner before the wire in the wall heated up enough to create a fire. The small filament would overheat first, tripping the fuse and taking pressure off the wiring inside the house, thus avoiding a bigger issue. Since this action also cut the power, the homeowner knew a fuse had blown and could identify which one by the cracked glass or black appearance.

While the circuit breaker in a modern panel box functions in the same way as the older fuses I've described, the new version is an electronic feature that can be reset instead of replaced. With the newer systems, the breaker trips when an issue arises, removing electricity from the line until something is unplugged or the breaker is reset. Continually resetting the breaker with the circuit overloaded may cause the breaker to trip repeatedly, burn out, and require replacement.

Modern panel boxes have two types of breakers that serve specialized functions. Similar to a standard breaker, the ground fault breaker keeps current flowing at a constant, safe draw. Since water conducts electricity and can cause electrocution, this breaker has a second function, interacting with the ground to provide a precaution in wet locations such as a bathroom or kitchen. If, at any point, the green ground wire comes in contact with water, it will immediately turn off the outlet.

> **Mark-It: While you may find several types of breakers in a panel box, it is important to understand the codes for your region, especially since they have changed in recent years.**

Ground Fault Circuit Interrupters (GFCIs)

In bathrooms, kitchens, and other wet areas, most municipalities also require ground fault circuit interrupters (GFCIs) that have a small button positioned within the outlet itself. This special outlet is performing the same function as the ground fault breaker in the panel box but it pops quicker because it is tripped at the source. By code, most inspectors require a GFCI outlet in each location where water is likely to interact with electricity. Depending on your jurisdiction, you may be required to change the ground fault in the panel box to these location-based outlets. Could you have both—one in the box and one in the bathroom? Yes, but there is no need to maintain a redundant system. Just remember that, if you only have the ground fault breaker in the box, you will likely be required to add GFCIs in wet areas within the house.

Arc Fault Circuit Interrupter (AFCI)

Another special breaker found in modern panel boxes is an arc fault circuit interrupter (AFCI). As you might remember from science class, when someone holds positive and negative prongs close together, electricity can jump or spark from one side to the other. The arc that shoots power from a positive to negative charge is basically releasing free-flowing electricity into the air. An electrical arc in your home is dangerous, with the power to kill. Remember, electricity is a circuit of positive and negative energy that flows like a river. When there is nothing plugged into an outlet, the current is at a standstill. If a serious arc issue occurs when you connect the appliance or bulb, electricity may complete the circuit and flow through *you*.

Given this potential danger, it's easy to see why arc faults are needed in new construction. Unlike the thick plaster walls used decades ago, today's drywall is thinner and more susceptible to punctures. Comprised of ⅜- or ½-inch thick sheetrock attached to a 2x4, new walls are easy to patch, making it common for people to hang pictures without hesitation. The problem is that wires are running unprotected inside the walls, providing an opportunity for screws, nails, or staples to accidentally puncture the positive and negative electrical wires.

While AFCIs used to be mandatory only in bedroom circuits, many counties have expanded the code to require everything in the panel box to be either a ground fault or an arc fault. The budget impact of this regulation is significant when standard $20 breakers must be replaced with specialized $80 to $150 components that will be expensive to install and maintain.

> **Mark-It**: In old home rehabs, AFCIs can present a challenge because they are overly sensitive.

For those of us in rehab, the sensitivity and ultimate impact of arc faults presents an even bigger dilemma than the cost of adding them. Of course, if I encounter a situation where there is evidence that a fire or other issue has caused damage, I would not hesitate to install AFCIs and replace all the wiring. However, while code may require AFCI updates in the panel box of a 40-year-old home, there may be no need to replace accompanying copper-insulated wiring that is in good condition. In cases such as this, there is a good chance that the newly-installed AFCI will continuously sense slight fluctuations in the older system and trip breakers unless all the wiring in the house is replaced. This illustrates the challenge of installing arc faults in a house that has been perfectly safe for 40-plus years.

I understand that we need to learn continuously and make homes safer as we go forward. Yet, difficulties may arise when we must keep pace with new advances—and still try to save a house. Sometimes, you can't have both. If I have to tear out the drywall and reconstruct the components, I might as well build a new house–which of, course, I could do. But I'd rather not. I'd prefer to save a cool, old house that we'll never see again without subjecting it to requirements that may have no impact for potential buyers.

A Wire Guide

As a rehabber or purchaser of an older home, it is important to understand the different wiring systems that have been used throughout the years. While many of these methods are perfectly acceptable, others require expensive removal and rework. Modernizing a home's electrical system can be costly, time-consuming, and labor intensive. Be sure to consider the budget impact and work investment.

> **Mark-It: Comprehensive rewiring projects usually require the demolition of wallboards and plaster to pull new wires. The new wiring work should be handled by a master electrician to ensure that it is installed correctly with proper permits.**

Here's a look at the types of wire you're likely to find in older homes, along with a recommended approach for each:

1) *Knob and tube system of fiber-covered wires:* Since these early systems had only positive and neutral wires with no ground, they will need to be removed and replaced. I don't recommend connecting any modern appliances to this antiquated system.

2) *Fabric-coated copper:* With the fabric coating serving as a sleeve, these wires were often run through a flexible, metal conduit for added protection against penetration by animals and other sources. While this type of system is unlikely to pose an imminent danger, there is no way to assess its condition, so I recommend replacement.

3) *Fabric-coated aluminum:* This lightweight and conductive material was used in the 1940s when copper was scarce during the war. Since it is not very dense, aluminum tends to heat up quickly when electricity flows through it. As a result, aluminum wiring is not used in modern construction because it can't handle the draw of today's robust appliances. A new microwave or hair dryer will put a strain on this lightweight metal, causing it to heat up like a light bulb and potentially cause a fire. Since we obviously don't want that to happen, I recommend that you remove aluminum wiring in most cases.

There is one rare situation when you may be able to leave aluminum wiring in place if it meets *all* of these conditions:

- It exclusively serves an overhead light fixture.
- It was installed correctly.
- It is in excellent condition.

With the invention of LED or complex fluorescent technology, today's light bulbs are more efficient and draw less power than older styles. If aluminum wiring to such an overhead light will be limited in its draw *with no potential to serve appliances,* it may be okay to leave in place. Just remember, if the aluminum wire runs to a regular outlet where you can't control what will be connected, it must always be removed.

The bigger issue with aluminum is that it is a highly sensitive metal that can set off a reaction when it comes in contact with copper.

Mark-It: **An aluminum wire should *never* be connected into a breaker or fixture with a copper screw.**

If a connection is needed, you must use screws and breakers that are specifically rated for aluminum. Most modern light fixtures and outlets have copper leads that cannot be attached to aluminum wires. These situations require special sealed connectors that eliminate contact between the aluminum and copper wires.

Here are some pointers for reworking a house with aluminum wiring:

- When adding a microwave in a kitchen where aluminum wiring previously existed, have the electrician pull a new copper line to the outlet from the breaker box. The same procedure applies for general outlets and new GFCIs where a hair dryer might be plugged in—anywhere you need to be sure the wire is sufficient for the load.

- Finding and identifying necessary changes can be time-consuming and costly. Past experience has proven that the expense and effort of having an electrician install a new panel box and wiring isn't much different from identifying and replacing all the specific areas that need attention. As a result, when I encounter a house with an aluminum system, I usually add a modern panel box with new wiring.

- It is critical to understand that Harry Homeowner may have unwittingly added copper screws in the wrong places. By the time you discover all the issues in the house you plan to rehab, you will likely determine that it is more cost effective, better for your sanity, and safer for the person buying the house to replace the aluminum wiring with modern copper. Be on the lookout for these issues—and for flippers that might miss these important details—leaving you susceptible to aluminum wiring pitfalls. Inspectors are helpful in identifying these concerns.

- Finally—and this is important—the person buying the house needs to understand where aluminum wiring exists in the house and how it can be used. Communicate all the issues.

4) *Plastic-coated copper.* As the challenges of aluminum escalated and copper again became available, electrical systems evolved to copper with a plastic coating. This style of wiring is cost-effective and safe, with a plastic coating that adheres directly to the copper. Less brittle than the old plastics, it has a longer lifespan and doesn't separate from the wire. Although it has the potential to melt if a circuit is overtaxed, safety measures have been added in new systems to alleviate this issue.

Get Grounded and Know Your Colors

Electrical systems should always be connected to the ground so there is a place for the power to go if there is arcing, contact with water, or some other malfunction. The ground neutralizes the electricity to prevent electrocution and other problems.

> **Mark-It**: **A ground wire can be identified by its green color, running along with the black, white, and sometimes red (for a switch or ceiling fan) wires within the plastic coating**.

In some older versions of Romex, the green ground wire was included with the other wires but not coated, since it was acting only as a conduit to move electricity to the ground. While this is common and perfectly acceptable, modern Romex wraps all wires inside a soft plastic casing, providing insulated protection if things heat up. When reviewing a house for purchase, look for this type of wiring to ensure the best use and safety.

I'll conclude the electrical section with a story about a ridiculous panel box I encountered years ago. As my first foray into the arc fault world, the nonsense that ensued almost made me get out of the rehab business altogether.

> It was obvious that the wiring in this particular house had been updated numerous times in the 1950s, creating a mishmash that is nearly impossible to describe. On the basement wall, I found a main power box with ample expansion space and existing copper wiring split in several directions. Adjacent to this main power box was an old, flip-by-hand breaker panel attached to wires extending from shotgun-shell fuses. In addition, there was a small subpanel with modern, trip-style breakers and two oddly-connected timers. The whole conglomeration was screwed to a plywood board attached to the wall. Was it dangerous? Maybe. But people had been using this convoluted system every day with no evidence of a fire and the house was now in foreclosure.
>
> Since the wiring was all copper, there were no issues with aluminum, but the panel box situation was something I did not want to explain to a buyer or home inspector. After determining that the wiring was modern with only a few insufficient circuits that could easily be replaced, I decided to install a new panel box and keep the existing system. This plan would allow me to connect everything to new breakers and GFCIs as needed. In addition, I would pull a few new lines for the microwave and electric dryer.
>
> The rehab went well and the house sold with relative speed. Then came the house inspection. My new panel box and fixtures were up to code, having been properly installed by the electrician before the permitting was changed to require AFCIs. Although arc faults were not required, the home inspector (who loved to wow people with his knowledge) told the buyers about the new arc fault technology, explaining that, in his opinion, their panel box should have them. Built to code at the time, the house was grandfathered, yet he told the buyers that everything should be changed. As any uninformed person in that situation would do, the buyers put their faith in the inspector to whom they had paid $550 for his two hours of time.

He used those two hours to compile an inspection report stating that all the breakers had to be replaced. Remember, this was a brand-new panel box with brand-new breakers that I was now required to remove and replace with AFCIs. I had followed proper procedures to ensure that the house was not dangerous, and knew that the addition of arc faults was likely to make the system more sensitive to tripping. I tried to make the agent understand that arc faults were not required and that they would constantly trip when used in conjunction with the existing wiring, even without a major arcing issue.

In this case, the inspector had convinced the buyers that I was the devil who bought the house cheap and was trying to soak them for as much money as possible. After spending $150,000 and seven months of my life to revive a treasure for a family to inhabit, I got lumped in with every flipper and half-baked Harry Homeowner in the minds of the buyers, inspector, and agent. No matter how I tried, I couldn't convince them of the truth: I rehabbed the house, brought it back to life, and did it the right way. Despite these efforts, the buyer thought I was trying to cheat my way out.

What choice did I have? Against my will, I replaced all the breakers with AFCIs. When I tested the system, as expected, the arc fault tripped every time a bathroom fan was turned on or the compressor for the bar refrigerator kicked in. Although I knew the buyers would be living in a house with constant breaker issues, there was nothing I could do about it.

When the ensuing home inspection took place, I received a phone call saying that the lights were not working in the basement and one other location. I instructed the buyers to flip the breaker at the panel box because the arc fault would constantly trip as long as both the refrigerator and bathroom fan were in use. When they said they couldn't live that way, I again explained the situation. Of course I ended up replacing newly installed breakers that cost $80-$150 with the original $20 standards. This is the stuff we go through so people can use refrigerators and bathroom fans at the same time.

I share these stories because I'm sure you'll encounter similar situations. It is important for people to understand that there are many honest rehabbers who are looking out for an owner's best interest. We are not dishonest and we're not evil. We are human beings. Yes, I'm in this business to make money but I also want each home to be an incredible, safe, long-term investment for a family. It is frustrating when inspectors automatically assume the worst from rehabbers and it is beyond hard for me to be lumped in with flippers.

Seven or More Degrees of Separation

From my perspective, it is frustrating that the homebuying process creates so many levels of separation between me and the buyers I'm trying to help. If you're looking for a car, you want to buy it from someone you trust. In real estate, I rarely get to establish such a relationship. Typically, the buyers are represented by an agent who writes their contract and talks to my agent who then talks to me. As you can see, any opportunity for me to communicate special details about the house is like a game of telephone. That's what happened in the story about arc faults. After candidly explaining the process to the agent and inspector, my story reached the buyers' ears this way: "He doesn't want to spend the time and money. He says you won't like it." Since they thought I had an attitude and didn't want to be bothered with extra work, the buyers lost trust.

The correct translation is powerful. Consider the impact of the inspector in this telephone game. Remember, the buyers' deposit check to the inspector was being held in escrow so they felt he was looking out for them. Often, buyers feel more allegiance to the inspector than to their agent who is paid by the seller. After all, they believe they are paying a construction professional to be in their corner. Inspectors feel obligated to deliver on this monetary relationship, working to provide $550-worth of advice and information. While I believe that most inspectors act in the best interest of the buyers, at times they confuse how to differentiate safe practices in older and newer homes. Inspection guidelines should consider these nuances. Perhaps, someday, they will.

Accessories Complete the Ensemble

A discussion of electricity would not be complete without the mention of light fixtures. This is an area where I never skimp. Light fixtures are the jewelry of a house—the necklace, earrings, or bracelet—that adorn it with style and class even when it is empty.

Mark-It: All the time and energy spent rehabbing a house to perfection is wasted if you install light fixtures that you found on a two-for-one table at a big box store.

Unless the original light fixtures are time-honored treasures, work with a designer, develop a theme that is worthy of the house, and invest in meaningful jewelry that people will notice. This isn't a hunch; my strategy is the result of conversations with numerous buyers who told me they fell in love with the home because of the lighting.

The rehab business is all about knowing where to invest assets. Sometimes light fixtures are more important than crown molding. You can take that to the bank.

CHAPTER 25

Everything Else

Now that we've discussed the main components of the house, I'll move on to mechanicals, appliances, and accessories. Since these features are not part of the main structure, they are easy to replace and should not make or break a deal.

Hassle-Free HVAC

Let's get the big one out of the way first: the HVAC system. Since it's nearly impossible to sell a rehabbed home that does not have central air and heating, this can be one of your most expensive budget add-ons. Many older homes are deficient in this area, requiring the installation of extensive ductwork to make them current and comfortable.

> **Mark-It**: In pursuing cost-effective heating and cooling options, start by contacting a licensed HVAC contractor who will conduct an analysis and provide an estimate.

If you encounter an older home that does not provide sufficient space for ducting, the HVAC contractor may recommend a ductless system of flexible, 3-inch pipes that are run through ceilings and walls to circular outlets in each room. Although these systems are relatively expensive, they work well and are easy to install without disrupting the character of a classic structure.

Boiler Systems

There are a variety of central heating systems, including radiant methods that run heated water through a wall-mounted or standing radiator. Boiler systems provide a viable method for home heating although some buyers are leery of them. Running off gas, electric, oil, or geothermal, the central boiler heats the water to create steam and pump it through a plumbing system. Expensive to install, this metal piping is separate from the home's hot water supply. As hot water is pumped through the pipes, radiated heat is delivered to each room. When warmer air is needed, the thermostat is turned up, heating the water to elevate the temperature. This system provides many benefits, including comfortable temperatures via radiant air movement. Most importantly, it delivers consistent humidity levels throughout the living areas, offering an optimal environment for people with allergies and sinus issues. In addition to providing advantages for humans, this type of heat benefits the living, breathing elements of the house, making hardwood floors and wood trim less susceptible to drying and cracking. Some forced-air systems attempt to accomplish this through the addition of costly humidity options.

Some disadvantages of a boiler system are the space occupied by radiators and the impact on room design. Several modifications have been made to overcome these issues, including the introduction of wall-mounted versions for those who don't want to live with their grandmother's version of a radiator under the window topped by a doily and plant. Baseboard styles have been modernized to blend with the trim, making them barely noticeable. In cold climates, radiant heat is a popular backup for a forced-air system, providing an optimal warming source that does not dry out everything and everyone in the house.

> **Mark-It: Learn about the benefits of boiler systems; many of the newly-designed products have long lifespans that rival other methods.**

A forced-air heating system is separate from central air, although traditionally they share the same ductwork. In some cases, central air may have been added to a home where the heat is still supplied through a radiator system. This is fine as long as the ducting is modern, efficient, and capable of handling the living areas.

Centralized Systems

Today, it is common to combine air conditioning and heating into a centralized system. In the furnace portion, heat may be generated via a gas or oil burner that functions like a chafing dish with a flame that heats a tray of water to warm the food. A gas or oil furnace follows the same principle by using fire to heat an element through which air is pushed. To eliminate emissions into the house, the exhaust is then discharged through an insulated pipe and out a chimney. The electric system is cleaner, functioning more like a toaster with coils that heat up as the air blows across them. With no emissions, this system creates air that is forced out of the ducts. This is also how emergency heat works on a basic heat pump.

Heat Pumps

Functional and efficient, heat pumps are prevalent in areas that are not prone to extreme cold temperatures. While they have standard air conditioning coils to cool the air, the only warmth generated by a heat pump comes from the emergency electrical system described above, which is rarely used and expensive to run. The concept behind a heat pump is that it has an exchanger that functions like an air conditioner in reverse. Air conditioning uses a compressor to pump refrigerant through a coil and into a system of tubes. The circulating system continuously moves air through the compressor and across the coils to keep the environment cool.

Reversing this methodology, the heating system pumps gas in the other direction. Instead of the warmer gas going outside the house to the condenser, it is pumped through the interior unit. While not hot, this gas remains at a warmer room temperature. Since it typically only warms to about 68 to 70 degrees, this is why a heat pump is not preferred in regions of extreme cold.

Mark-It: If I am rehabbing a home with a boiler furnace that does not provide central air, I will often maintain the existing system as an emergency backup for extreme cold weather. I then install a heat pump system to provide central air and efficient heating that will keep the home at a comfortable temperature during the bulk of the year.

While this type of backup system is common in cold climates, baseboard heating is an easier but less efficient option.

Right-size the Water Heater

A water heater is nothing more than a giant pot of boiling water that pumps liquid into the plumbing system. The water is heated in a process that is very similar to boiling it on a stove. The tank—a pot or vessel inside a round cylindrical tube—is heated by an electrical element or via a fire ignited by gas, oil, or propane. Think of the cylinder as a giant thermal coffee pot holding water at a given temperature determined by a gauge.

Mark-It: I've noticed that many homes have water tanks that are undersized. Since a water heater doesn't last long and is relatively inexpensive, I usually budget to replace it unless it was installed in the last five years. An inspector will likely raise this issue anyway so you can avoid an annoyance on your punch list by handling it beforehand.

Although a water heater is a simple appliance and not particularly dangerous, you should avoid storing flammable objects near its heating element. Filled with water and prone to rust, the water heater has a limited lifespan. The problem occurs when people keep water heaters too long, until they rust, leak, and create an unexpected flood. Newer versions feature expansion tanks and/or pipes that channel leaks into a drain to help homeowners avoid this type of damage.

Appliances

I won't spend a lot of time on kitchen appliances since they vary significantly by function, price, and personal preferences. Changes in features and technology happen so quickly that many of my recommendations may be outdated by the time you read this.

> **Mark-It: When it comes to kitchen appliances, I usually include the most advanced technology available in stainless steel unless the house design requires a particular style.**

I've said it before and I'll say it again. If you encounter a vacant house and the power is off, never, ever, ever, EVER open a refrigerator or freezer of any kind. Tape it shut and get it out. I have seen and smelled things in refrigerators that I still can't un-see and un-smell. If you come across a refrigerator that is clean and you want to keep it, more power to you. I'm taking no more chances.

Kitchen appliances are like personal property so by the time a house makes it to me, they are often gone. If you encounter older dishwashers, microwaves, and ranges, it makes sense to replace them unless they are in pristine condition or super high end, like a Viking range. Luxury appliances that were custom-created for a specific kitchen may be worth a repair, but most standard models should be discarded and replaced. No one wants a new kitchen with old appliances and, as much as we all love recycling, there is almost no market for reselling or donating them. If you are purchasing a rehabbed property with mediocre appliances that were not replaced, you can assume the seller was cutting corners. Consider this a telltale sign of more deficiencies to come.

Be Adventurous

For rehabbers, the kitchen is a good place to invest money and deliver the latest home benefits. Be creative; many kitchen updates can be accomplished in a cost-effective way. There are always new advances in appliances and I like to incorporate them into my rehabbed kitchens. For example, refrigerators have evolved from the traditional freezer on top, to the freezer at bottom, to side-by-side with water and ice in the door, to the French-door style with multiple drawers below.

> **Mark-It: Although refrigerators aren't cheap, leave room in your budget for a state-of-the-art version that will wow buyers. For a sleek, built-in impression without extra cost,**

consider installing a counter-depth refrigerator with space-saving efficiency.

Microwaves continue to evolve with new versions that use less power, heat more quickly, and combine convection cooking for crisping foods like pizza. In addition to undergoing technological changes, the microwave (and the tiny cabinet above it) has moved away from its position over the stove, allowing the range hood of the 1970s to make a comeback. This trend has opened up an interesting space for artistic tile designs over the stove.

How does the microwave fit into the new kitchen design? There are several options. Some are wall unit styles built into the cabinets to accommodate a standard microwave. Others have been downsized from 16 inches to a more practical 12 and are installed in the cabinet run under the countertop. While this location may seem awkward at first, it is safer for homeowners than constantly reaching over a stovetop. Easily accessible, the under-counter or in-drawer microwave is located away from the main kitchen triangle, facilitating the simultaneous use of the space by multiple people.

> **Mark-It:** Incorporating the new microwave layout into my recent rehabs has allowed me to include a front-controlled range with space for incredible glass and tile art above. Most people say they never used that little cabinet above the stove for much of anything anyway—except as storage for the obligatory turkey platter.

Ranges, too, have evolved, with double-oven compartments that allow you to cook at two different temperatures without surrendering additional cabinet space. Cooktops are more functional and easier to clean, with a variety of accessories such as large and narrow burners, warmers, and induction heating. The slide-in range now offers front-oriented controls as an alternative to the inconvenient ones at the back of the stove. The appeal of appliances has been further enhanced with LED lighting that makes them more attractive, efficient, and easy to maintain.

Whenever possible, I include a beverage center for juice boxes, sodas, beer, wine, and other drinks. This isn't necessarily a bar; it is a designated area with an undercounter refrigerator for easy access.

> **Mark-It**: **Remember the old kitchen desks that were popular in the 1990s? No longer needed, this space has become the ideal area to repurpose as a cost-effective beverage center.**

You can replace the 24-inch cabinet with a counter-height refrigerator, resulting in a cost-effective tradeoff. The adjustable-height refrigerator is vented below and requires only a standard outlet, making it easy to install. To display barware, add a door cabinet above with interesting glass and include a sink if space allows. The beverage center location allows people to pop into the kitchen and grab a drink without disrupting activity in the workspace triangle comprised of the sink, refrigerator, and stove.

Washers and Dryers

Home buyers seem to view laundry appliances differently across the county. Here in the mid-Atlantic, people tend to leave washers and dryers in the house, while they are viewed as personal property in other geographic areas. Get to know what is standard in your region and be sure to disclose this properly on the contract so people know what to expect.

> **Mark-It**: **Even when well-maintained washers or dryers are left in a house, it may not be worth the effort to keep them because people get skittish about cleaning their clothes in used appliances.**

If your budget allows, install the latest efficient models or leave them out altogether. Front load washers have been trending, although mold issues related to the inside seal have limited their popularity. While this problem is easily avoidable if consumers dry the seal and leave the door open to eliminate moisture build-up, I don't think this concern will easily go away.

Perhaps more important than the appliances themselves is the room in which the washer and dryer are located. As homes have developed, the laundry area migrated from outside the house to the basement, finally landing in the main living area. Today, a fully-functional mudroom adds tremendous benefits, with a laundry facility, coat closet, shoe storage, benches, and more. Front-loaded appliances allow for counter space and cabinets above, creating functional and aesthetically pleasing elements.

> **Mark-It: Plan to create a mudroom/laundry area with ample storage whenever possible.**

No One Wants a Used Toilet

Fixtures such as tubs, sinks, and toilets are parts of the plumbing system that I almost always replace. Efficiencies change and old styles will quickly date a room. Unless the house has a golden toilet or a unique detail from the 1950s, there is no reason to keep existing fixtures even if they are only a few years old. Ceramic sinks, tubs, and toilets are natural products that may be broken up and taken to a landfill.

> **Mark-It: When installing new fixtures, I almost always choose white, a look that will remain bright and classic without fading. If you want to get creative in the bathroom, leave the fixtures alone and do it with tile.**

Get Down to Flooring

It's easy to estimate flooring on a square-foot basis and for budget purposes, this is almost always included as a replacement unless existing hardwood can be refinished. Hardwood on the main level is preferred by most buyers so plan to add it if it's not already there. Find a professional flooring contractor who knows what he or she is doing. With a variety of installation techniques, it's important to use the installation method that matches the product.

> **Mark-It: If you cheap out and buy wood off the shelf with a DIY installer, you will screw it up. Trust me.**

When it comes to purchasing carpet, this is where many flippers fail. Finding themselves behind schedule, they order carpet off a roll, even if it doesn't fit the home's overall design. Build time into your schedule and order product in advance. Never use builder-grade carpet; always step it up at least one notch. I use upgraded padding under medium grade carpet and it works like a charm. It looks fantastic, feels great, and will stand the test of time.

> **Mark-It: Make it your goal to find good carpet at a reasonable price rather than cheap carpet at a quick price.**

Rather than a pile, I select a low mat—sometimes with a neutral pattern—that will provide flexibility for interior schemes. To avoid a dated look, use gray as a neutral rather than beige. This holds true for most of the interior décor. As a designer at heart, I spend a lot of time reviewing materials and choosing the right ones for each specific project. The time investment is worth it when all the pieces come together.

> **Mark-It: Avoiding vinyl, I often install ceramic or porcelain in baths, venturing beyond the obligatory 12x12 tiles.**

Depending on the location, I'll try an elongated tile or a new trend such as wood-look ceramic. Ceramic or porcelain elements may also be used in the kitchen although I believe hardwood will make that space look larger and create a more contiguous flow.

Ways to Wow Them

Little things matter. When it comes to creating memorable homes, I have a few tricks up my sleeve, such as adding Bluetooth fans with nightlights in the bathroom that can be connected to a smartphone to play music through a ceiling-mounted speaker. Who doesn't like to listen to music while in the shower or attending to every other task that happens in a bathroom?

> **Mark-It: Based on the comments I receive, it's obvious that everyone likes gadgets. I know that one well-implemented idea can separate my home from the pack.**

My other signature features include adding USB ports, charger stations, and dimmer switches in key locations throughout the house as well as using only LED bulbs to make homes as cost efficient as possible. These ideas come from thinking about how people truly live in a house, day in and day out. The small additions may seem trivial—and, yes, they increase the budget—but I always include them because they make my properties memorable when compared with the ten other homes people will tour in one weekend. Now that I mentioned this in print, everyone will be doing it so I'll have to come up with some new ideas.

PART FIVE

THE ADVENTURE

*Yeah, you really can turn a lifelong passion
into a purpose.*

CHAPTER 26

Flipping Out or Flipping Off

I didn't set out to be an author. It happened when I realized that I can't fulfill my vocation without helping people understand what rehabbing truly is. By now, you've probably begun to form your own perceptions of flippers and rehabbers. It's time to determine where you fit into the spectrum. What type of business is right for you? Or, as a future owner, what type of rehabbed home do you want to buy? The answer to these questions may be found in the type of person you are in your everyday life.

If you like get-rich-quick schemes, you might be attracted to the idea of flipping houses. With a focus on cost-cutting and turn-around rather than quality and craftsmanship, marginal renovations are often dumped in the laps of unsuspecting, uneducated buyers. If, on the other hand, you value hard work, have integrity, and want to save houses the right way, you have the makings of a genuine rehabber.

Surprisingly, in order to discover where your rehab path leads, I suggest that you start by taking a look *back*. Is there a pattern in your background, experiences, desires, and talents? Do you have an appreciation for houses, projects, workmanship, and design? Whether you are interested in rehabbing homes or living in a remodeled treasure of your own, this requires a mentality that transcends a simple real estate transaction.

The Real Truth About the American Dream

Let me address those of you who are thinking of setting up residence in a rehabbed home. People often say that home ownership is the American dream. Like so many things in life, we are brainwashed to feel a certain way about this concept through TV shows and pop culture. It's no different than going to college or getting married. Society tells us there are things we are supposed to do as human beings. The truth is, there is no predetermined course. You don't have to think or feel a certain way. Do some soul searching before you jump in. Dig deep. If you discover that you truly don't want to own a home—or you only want it because everyone wants you to want it— then face your fear and change course.

As humans, we are born with two innate fears: the fear of falling and the fear of loud noises. Most of our worries—like being afraid of spiders or home ownership—are the result of influence from our parents or society. Our joys, interests, talents, and concerns are learned. The quest for the American dream is caught up in this concept. Somewhere along the line, we've been taught that home ownership matters. What they didn't teach us is that being a homeowner is a pain in the ass—and anyone who owns a home knows this. There is no such thing as a maintenance-free house or a home that is perfect. If you are mega-wealthy, with caretakers for everything, then your ideal home might exist. For the rest of us, the American dream has flaws.

Houses are not perfect things. They never will be. They are living, breathing entities. When you decide to buy a rehabbed house, it's like deciding you want a dog or a child—on a different scale. The family house will likely be your biggest material expense and taking care of it is hard. If that concept is not for you, it's okay. Despite what society says, there's nothing wrong with renting an apartment or buying a condo to avoid the work and headaches. Let's face it; if you don't care to know how the water gets to your sink or where it goes when you flush, you have choices. You can live in a condo and let someone else take care of things that need to be repaired, painted, or mowed. There's nothing wrong with not wanting to own a pain-in-the-ass house. So don't let society brainwash you into owning a dream that, for you, would be a nightmare.

An Authentic Rehab is the Puppy You Got From the Shelter Instead of the Pet Store

If soul searching does lead you to the American dream, the next step is to determine whether you are a good match for a salvaged house. Rehabbed houses are quirky, and that is what makes them wonderful. Like every rescued puppy out there, rehabbed houses are lovably unique. While a pure-bred dog and newly-constructed home both look great on paper, each may fall short on the long-term happiness scale. If you continuously look for faults in a house, puppy, or the world around you, don't be surprised when you find them. Rescued homes are a good match for people who appreciate the beauty in time-honored materials while accepting the fact that people, puppies, and products are fallible. A good rehabber will prepare you for these realities with full disclosure. You'll understand that even if your rescued pup drools a bit, with tender loving care he will be loyal for years.

> *This reminds me of a movie called Baby Boom. The story starts after a family member passes away and the main character, played by Diane Keaton, decides to buy a place in the country to raise a young child that has been left in her care. What is memorable about this movie is Diane Keaton's line after she has undergone numerous problems with the house, finally encountering a monumental issue in the kitchen. When the contractor explains the need to dig a new well and install an expensive new system, she melts down, saying, "I don't want to know where the water comes from, I just want to turn on the faucet and have it there."*

If you are like Diane Keaton in this movie, then a life of rehabbing—or living in a rehabbed home—will be difficult. On the other hand, if you want to understand the details, be part of the solution, and unleash a home's potential, then maybe you've discovered something more.

Once you know that a rescued home is right for you, perfection will take on a new meaning. Seek a rehabber who shares your vision. Like many other professionals in this industry, I incorporate a part of myself into every home I deliver. I don't cut corners, instead doing everything possible to make a home enjoyable, functional, safe, and beautiful.

As a person who has spent most of my life in the customer service industry, I've been trained to create things that speak to the masses. In department stores, I designed environments to engage customers and encourage them to buy. I crafted ways to help people feel comfortable enough to trust the seller and make a purchase. When I relate this piece of my background to the work I do now, I realize that I've always been focused on helping people find things they truly want. As rehabbers, our main responsibility is to make people happy—we just have to find the right people. Remember, not everyone is worthy to be the owner of an adorable, rescued house.

A trip to the dentist illustrates the customer happiness challenge.

> *Going to the dentist has to be one of the world's most miserable customer satisfaction situations. The best dentist can hire talented hygienists, have a beautiful office, provide fantastic service, and use the latest technology, but the bottom line is, people don't like squirming in a dental chair and spending money on teeth. In fact, we hate going to the dentist. If you think about it, teeth only require minor maintenance, but when parents get busy, kids eat too much candy, and everyone forgets to floss, a trip to the dentist is unavoidable. No matter how nice the dentist is, this isn't a trip to Disney World, so we go begrudgingly, knowing it will be uncomfortable for both mouth and wallet. Unless, perhaps, the dentist is Jennifer Aniston in that movie Horrible Bosses ... but that's another story.*

> *After going to the dentist, we'll question how we got three cavities, complain about the deductible, worry that the insurance doesn't cover more, and ask for a second opinion on a root canal. We'll come up with a million reasons to dislike a top-notch dentist who has a five-star rating. Because, unfortunately, a dentist is not part of that American dream. Once we have neglected our teeth, a dentist is a necessary evil that cannot satisfy us, regardless of her effort. We'll go to another dentist, get the same answers, and continue to be frustrated. The dentist is used to this, so she can only smile and move on to the next patient. She'll try to make the experience as tolerable as possible even though she knows it may be difficult for us.*

Like teeth that need to be maintained, a house requires attention. This won't change, regardless of how pretty, nice, and livable I make it. A home will always demand love and care. On top of that, unexpected things will happen. I can't prevent the unprecedented cold snap that will cause a pipe to burst and flood the carpet a week after settlement when the new owners are away on vacation. Regardless of all the permitting and inspections, there is nothing I can do about the limited lifespans of expensive mechanical systems. Despite all of this, I work hard to provide a unique, desirable product that can't be replicated.

Houses actually aren't that much like teeth, after all. You have choices. No one is forcing you into a rehab. Have a heart-to-heart talk with yourself and be prepared for the responsibility that comes with your decision to purchase a rescued home. When I deliver a house to you, I'm giving you the best product I can provide at the moment. I will make every effort to safeguard it from the elements and prepare it for the future. Yet, no matter how much research and work I put into it, tomorrow is another day. I've learned to do my best, provide relentless follow up, and move on knowing I gave it my all. If something goes wrong, it's not because I cut corners. In fact, the opposite is true.

CHAPTER 27

Bob Vila vs. Anything on HGTV

My book would not be complete without some words about Bob Vila, a pioneer in this industry who hosted *This Old House* starting in the 1970s. Unlike today's home improvement hosts, Bob Vila had no fancy studio, camera crew, or sponsors; he was just doing his thing on public TV like the happy little landscape artist. Bob Vila was a real guy, not some TV personality running around at dinner parties and shows. As a true craftsman, he was knowledgeable, creative, and knew the ins and outs of rehab.

One of the ways Bob Vila demonstrated his intelligence was by acknowledging the things he *didn't* know. He hired experts for detail work, asking them a million questions we all wanted answers to. Recognizing the beauty and strength of manmade creations, Bob Vila was clearly focused on showing people how to preserve the past and save our heritage. Instead of throwing homes away, he wanted to show people how to lovingly put them back together again.

Bob Vila wasn't nasty or sharp-edged, but he also wasn't a made-for-TV celebrity persona with jokes built into his dialogue. He was the narrator of a documentary who asked legitimate questions and laughed about real things. He was, in essence, a shop teacher inviting us into an authentic classroom. Filmed before the days of instant gratification, video wasn't edited to make it look like projects happened in fifteen minutes and the crew didn't remove irrelevant stuff.

Instead of looking for outrageously unique projects, Bob Vila chose houses with problems we could relate to so he could take us along on the journey and provide solutions. We were invited to follow a house rehab from start to finish. It wasn't a half-hour glimpse at a different house each week hosted by a couple with an oddball relationship. It was just Bob Vila, the contractors, and a project. It was so easy to learn things the right way from him because he never cut corners; he was always working to discover the best method. He would ask: Is this product going to last? If we have to redo this, will it stay true to the original building? It seemed that he would only upgrade materials or add cost-efficient systems if it didn't change the character of the project at hand.

If I had to associate myself with anyone on TV who matches my rehab perspective, it would be Bob Vila. As an impressionable kid making my way through the 1970s and 1980s, I related to his genuine perspective. Through Bob Vila, I absorbed a passion for houses that inspired youthful sketches before developing into formal education and a lifelong career. I will always retain the fundamentals learned from this authentic pioneer in the industry. If you haven't watched Bob Vila's shows, dig them up, especially if you want to become a rehabber. Even though the show was produced decades ago, I guarantee you will learn something of value—including how much you don't know.

There is no comparison between shows like *This Old House* and modern productions. Today's versions come in all shapes and sizes, featuring mother-daughter teams, brothers, spouses, and more. This insanity will eventually go away when they run out of material, angles, and crazy characters. Of today's personalities, the ones that most closely match my perspective are Chip and Joanna Gaines from *Fixer Upper*. Compared with most of the other made-for-TV nonsense, they seem to actually know what they are doing. They tackle projects that are similar in condition to those I see in my market. Usually, they'll tour two or three decrepit mid-centuries or farm houses with closed floorplans that don't work for today's families. Chip and Joanna convey an innate ability that is vital to being a successful rehabber: they connect with people and help them see the possibilities.

Unlike most other rehab hosts, Chip and Joanna tend to identify issues early on—such as plumbing problems, rotten floor joists, and insect infestations—giving people a realistic vision of what to expect in terms of time and cost. While some unpleasant surprises may still occur along the way, they professionally address issues with the buyers. If a larger problem arises or the promised budget is not met, Chip and Joanna sometimes work out a solution themselves rather than showing the buyers how ridiculous it was that they didn't find it earlier. While some TV rehabbers view the buyers as an endless pot of money, Joanna often includes a contingency for surprise upgrades. My contingency is 10%, and when it is not needed, I use the amount to knock the cover off the ball with an additional light fixture or unexpected detail. Sometimes the contingency ends up as pure profit. If you don't add this flexibility into your budget, you can expect, at times, to be screwed.

With the original purpose of educating people about home projects, HGTV has become an entertainment enterprise designed to keep you tuned in. If you think all the scenarios on TV are 100% real, you will be sorely disappointed when you quit your job and dump your money into a rehab project.

As an up-and-coming rehabber, your path may be completely different from mine. The important thing is to discover where yours is leading. I didn't wake up one day and decide to get into the business after watching a TV show. A lifelong journey of experiences led me to where I am. Whatever you do, please don't call me a flipper. Twenty years ago, we wouldn't have given the word "flipper" a second thought. In fact, it was the name of a popular TV show about a beloved dolphin. Yet, today, I wouldn't want to be called a flipper any more than Bob Vila or Chip and Joanna Gaines would. At least I don't think they would, although I don't know them any better than you do.

If Bob and Chip and Joanna and I aren't flippers, then what are we? I believe we are surgeons, rehabbers, and savers of homes. We are in the renewal business, bringing the past to life.

CHAPTER 28

The Money Pit

Before you read this next section, you have an assignment. Go watch *The Money Pit*. If you've already seen it, watch it again with your rehab hat on. I agree that the movie is dated. Nobody dresses like that anymore. But, in Hollywood-style, Shelley Long and Tom Hanks nail the homeownership concept of expecting the unexpected. The exaggerated plot manages to provide a realistic view of the challenges you might face in hiring contractors to help you save a neglected, dilapidated house.

Since I know a lot of you won't take the time to watch the movie, I'll share my interpretation. The plot begins when an urban couple is lured by the fantasy of getting their dream home at a dreamy price. As New York City apartment dwellers, they have no idea what it takes to own, maintain, and live in a house, so they trust their shyster real estate friend when he says, "Have I got a deal for you."

As it turns out, this isn't just any home. It's a classic colonial that needs a ton of work and is being unloaded in some sort of desperation sale. The couple's first impression of the property is misleading. They see a spacious living space wrapped with pretty ribbons in a picturesque setting at an unbelievable price. Not wanting to miss out on such a value, they buy it while refusing to acknowledge copious red flags. Seeing that the plumbing is a disaster, they rationalize how they will compensate by using only the main floor bathroom. There are rooms they don't go into and important things amiss, including a staircase that becomes a disastrously funny focal point. When the sales consultant tells them to "watch your step," it foreshadows something much bigger than the small repair she describes. Throughout the tour, the naïve buyers are blinded by the agent's sensational description of the house and its classic furnishings.

> *Note to reader:* You've heard me preach about this. Don't get sucked in by amazing architectural details, wonderful woodworking, or an agent's pretty property presentation. Do your research, heed the warning signs, and develop a budget—before you buy. If you see something, hear something, or smell something, there probably *is* something. Understand it and deal with it—or do a 180.

Our unsuspecting couple buys the house without raising concerns, without getting an inspection, and without negotiating the price while their friendly sales agent munches on jelly doughnuts. The money needed to buy and fix up the house is obtained through questionable sources. Walter, played by Tom Hanks, borrows from a singer he represents as an accountant. Shelley Long's character, Anna, borrows from an ex-lover which of course creates interesting innuendo about favors related to the funding source.

> *Note to reader:* We've talked about funding sources. Don't be tempted to borrow from someone you haven't vetted 100%— and, please, not from questionable entanglements. Understand your options when it comes to hard money lenders. If you skipped that chapter, this would be a good time to read it.

Once the purchase is complete, the new owners pack some things and move right in, without cleaning rooms, checking systems, or repairing glitches. They soon discover that the house is literally falling apart. That doesn't make it less beautiful—it just makes it more real. This is where the movie earns its stripes as a comedy. The front door falls in, the doorbell malfunctions, and a faulty electrical wire causes a turkey to blow out of the oven while Julia Child talks about cooking on TV. When the house has no water, the resourceful couple fetches it from a fountain in the back yard, heating it on the stove to fill the bath. Of course the tub falls right through the rotted floor, launching a never-ending series of disastrous house-related escapades. When the staircase collapses into the foyer and they have to use a ladder to access their second-floor bedroom, the owners finally accept the fact that the house is falling apart. And, yes, that means they need to borrow more money.

> *Note to reader:* If our happy homeowners had done their research, they would have had choices. They could have borrowed the correct amount to complete the rehab or bought a different house altogether. Now that they're locked in, it will cost them more in the long run—and we're not just talking about money.

After accepting the fact that their dream home is a disaster, the desperate owners need contractors. As you might expect, most of the local pros are wise to this house and wouldn't touch it with a 10-foot pole. Trying to save money, the couple finally finds a few sub-par contractors who drive up in their expensive cars, make snide comments, and refuse to start without a deposit. After hearing what it will cost to correct the house they realize that, not only is the house a disaster, they are completely in over their heads. Now they need to borrow serious money.

> *Note to reader:* This is a good time to point out the benefit of understanding the story of a house before you buy. Talk to a local agent who knows the scoop, get an inspection, and do your own research. The house you're considering could have been on the market for six years or it might have been condemned. If you know these things, you won't find yourself in a situation like Anna and Walter.

The owners soon learn how true it is that you get what you pay for. As construction begins, each contractor tells them how long it will take to complete the work. When deadlines aren't met and workers are questioned repeatedly, the answer is always "two weeks." Like a parrot, this phrase is repeated over and over in the movie—until weeks become months.

Note to reader: In reality, when you ask painters, plumbers, electricians, and other contractors how long it will take to do a job, you are likely to hear "two weeks." I think this is some sort of unwritten, agreed-upon code. The bottom line is that, whether it takes two weeks or two months, they will finish on their schedule regardless of how much you jump up and down. Over time, you may provide enough business to attract contractors that will work exclusively for you but remember these are independent business owners working to make the quickest profit. Understand your holding costs and know that, no matter how hard you work to develop a plan, once you write the check to get a contractor started the schedule may become meaningless if he has to juggle numerous projects. Despite your best efforts, contractors will come in and out of your project as their time allows. The sooner you accept this, the happier you will be. You will make your life a living hell if you scream at the contractors and demand something they cannot deliver. They will walk off the job, leaving you in a no-win situation because no other contractors will want to come in and fix another guy's mess. If they do, the cost will be two or three times more than you would have paid in the first place. Your schedule is a balancing act. You need to have it, but there is an art to managing it.

Now that the contractors are working on their own schedules, they've basically taken up residence with Walter and Anna, like guests overstaying their welcome. In the movie, these laborers are portrayed as a weird cast of characters working on the house. No one knows if or when they will show up. A promise of Tuesday can turn into another day altogether. In one scene, when the owners tell a contractor that they didn't expect him that day, he replies with "Your number came up" as if he pulled a number out of a hat that led him to their house. While construction continues, the permitting process is portrayed as crooked, ridiculous, and filled with bribes.

Note to reader: Face the fact that the inspectors and people in the permit office are in control and most seem to enjoy flaunting their power. If you don't follow all the rules, fill out the correct forms, and meet them when they show up, they will deny your permits. That might mean waiting another three weeks for an appointment. Of course the movie exaggerates the process, but it's not that far off.

Three or four months later, we pick up the story with questionable contractors working in the house and the couple trying to live amid the chaos. Things seem to be moving along and work is being done, albeit not on schedule. There is an excitement level when the new stairway is installed and Walter can see light at the end of the tunnel. Yet, the house renovation has taken a toll on both people. They have become frustrated, grumpy, and irritated with each other. As these issues escalate, they decide to dissolve their partnership, finish the house, and sell it. Although it wasn't the plan at the beginning, the house purchase ultimately became a rehab—or actually, a flip.

> *Note to reader:* This illustrates why partnerships are often difficult in the rehab business. There will always be differences of opinion regarding what to fix, when to move forward, and how much money to spend—unless one is the backer and the other is running the business. There could be tension and repercussions causing one associate to walk away, leaving the other holding the bag. Give thought to these things before you establish your business.

As the project culminates in the movie, we begin to see the true beauty of the house. Having come to grips with the investment required for completion, the couple gains a clearer view of what it takes to build something worthwhile—whether it is a house or a relationship. This point, of course, is the underlying theme of the movie. Although it may be taxing and troublesome, the end result of doing something right can be a beautiful thing.

No spoiler alert needed—I won't give the entire ending away—because I still want you to watch the movie. But one line is worth sharing. As the general contractor hands the keys over to the couple he says, "You got lucky. If the foundation is good, everything else can be fixed."

> *Note to reader:* I believe in this line and say it all the time. Isn't that true about our relationships, our lives, our homes, and everything we do? If we embark on a situation, relationship, or project for the right reasons, are clear about why we're doing it,

and realistic about how we can get there, isn't it true that we can make things right—and put them back together if needed?

As we learn in the movie, if a house has a solid structure, it can all be repaired. It just requires time, money, and effort. Even after renovation, a rehabbed house needs understanding, energy, and maintenance. By today's standards, I would say that, done right, a rehabbed house may require less attention and anxiety than a new house because someone has already identified its quirks and eccentricities.

What's the bottom line? Don't lose your sense of humor. There are days when I have to tell myself to stay the course despite the stuff I face, the things inspectors find, the challenges contractors provide, and the questions buyers ask. Don't put yourself through the stress of becoming a rehabber or buying a rescued home unless you can laugh through the madness.

CHAPTER 29

Don't Let a Moral Dilemma Dampen Your Morale

Through the years, I've discovered that the time and effort required to maintain a home's beauty corresponds with the extent invested in the original creation. This circumstance is true of the simplest mid-century or the most intricate Victorian. Each one requires a unique attention to detail. No manner of renewal can change how the structures were conceived or what alterations they endured. Older homes stand as a tribute to the past, anchored in a time that is no longer here. In many cases, these houses have spectacular features that challenge current codes and defy modern technology.

Consider the transformation of an antique car that is restored to its original color and detail. Not only is it a tribute to a time period, the car actually becomes the restorer's best version of what it was originally meant to be. For true collectors, this adherence to authenticity enhances the vehicle's value. Yet, that car will not have the latest fuel economy, safety features, airbags, LED bulbs, or XM radio. In fact, it may not even have a radio. The restored car's value and beauty are rooted in the care that was taken to rebuild it. Even if it were refurbished with meticulous detail, the car may require more attention, refuse to start on cold days, or drip a bit of oil now and then. That doesn't mean the car is less valuable, beautiful, or desirable. It just requires a different kind of care.

This is how I view each rescued home that reflects the character and curb appeal of its original construction. As a rehabber, I can replace components, replicate details, and make the house seem brand ncw— but the truth is, it will never again be new. It will always be a restored creature in need of more love, care, and attention than a newly-built house.

This is my moral dilemma. I'm selling something that looks like new when I know it will require a lifetime of special care. I am continuously faced with the challenge of making sure my buyers understand this concept without scaring them away. Regardless of my enthusiasm for this business, I am not a miracle worker. Constrained by time and budgets, I do what I can to save a neglected structure for a new generation to enjoy. Yet, if the home's new family doesn't understand the kind of attention it needs, the two will never be compatible, let alone happy. If you become a devoted rehabber, you are likely to grapple with this dilemma, just as I do.

Rehabbing requires an abundance of patience. When an inspector says my breakers aren't up to code or a buyer expresses concern about the HVAC system, I do my best to listen to concerns, accommodate requirements, and mitigate dangers. I am always a teacher, helping buyers balance excitement with responsibility as they nurture a time-honored treasure.

CHAPTER 30

Bringing It Home

I built a career in home rehabilitation on a foundation of childhood hobbies and a structure of life experiences. It didn't happen overnight, and it wasn't the result of an episode I watched on HGTV. It was stirring inside me from an early age.

Ironically, I became a keenly visual person because at the beginning, I could barely see. Later, a random encounter with bulletin boards evolved into a 30-year department store career. And there is no doubt that I can trace my love of architecture back to the days of finding run-down structures and reinventing them in my drawings.

Looking back on the summer I spent renovating a house at biology camp in southern Maryland, perhaps science played a more important role than I realized. After many years of dissecting the experience and peeling back the layers, I can now see how many doors were opened. It was my first cut at self-reliance, self-preservation, self-motivation, and making my own way in the world. I learned how to cope, be alone, endure a panic attack, and see beyond the tired, old surface of a house. With all those layers exposed, it was one of the best experiences of my life.

In fact, it defined me.

The places we call home are spectacular things. As I look simultaneously back and forward, my thoughts center on this concept. A home is a living, breathing creature with countless moving parts. Crafted from human hands, each one has been willed into existence by our own ingenuity.

Perhaps, one day, someone will walk through one of my houses and talk about the guy who saved it and gave it another 50 or 100 years of life so a new family could nurture it into the future. And perhaps their children will stay there to witness another turn of the century. I won't be here for that—but, if I have anything to do with it, the house will.

It was a giant leap of faith to turn a lifelong passion into a vocation. The first step was the hardest, and the rest have been an adventure. Like many of us, I want to use my talent to leave a mark on this world. Ironically, that's my name—Mark—so I should have understood this from the start. As it turned out, it took me 50 years.

What's in your rearview mirror? Dare to look back, change course, and go after it.

ACKNOWLEDGMENTS

Many thanks to all my investors, big or small, because without you it would be impossible for me to do what I love. I'm especially grateful to those who were there for me in the beginning when funding was sometimes difficult to find.

This whole thing does not work without the right contractors … GCs, electricians, plumbers, HVAC, painters, landscapers and more. It takes time to find your match with the right ones, but once you are in sync, you can do great things together. I know, because I work with the best.

None of my vision would be possible without the right products and materials and the people who help me find them, match them, and put everything together. With so many options available today, you guys help me through the woods and lead me to just the right places.

Buying and selling real estate, especially here in Maryland, can be trying. Without the right team of people on your side you can quickly get yourself in trouble. Whether it's finding the right property to buy, determining the pricing strategy, or having the network of brokers and agents that work together to keep everything moving, this is essential to my business. I would especially like to single out Garceau Realty's Georgeanna Garceau, Dale Hevesy, and Donna Curry who get me through the days, the settlements, the problems, and the contracts. You are not just my co-workers; you are my friends.

My family and friends give me the ability to be away long days (sometimes working, sometimes not), support me when things don't go well (enduring my endless rantings), and listen as I talk about houses and work *all the time*. I could do none of this without you. Thank you for not putting constraints on my dreams and vision, but also for being there when I am disillusioned. Specifically, to my friend who insisted on being mentioned in the book, you'll have to read the whole thing to find your name. It's there.

Grandmom Bettie encouraged me to do the things I love and to be just who I am. She still inspires me today.

An endless number of people and businesses help me every day, including accountants, bookkeepers, caterers, attorneys, mortgage lenders, title companies, stagers, and on and on and on. Thank you. I never realized I would come to depend on you so much.

Thanks to Bruce Lenderking, who gave the book a test run before it was published. After that, I could see the finish line.

And to Eleni Makris, thank you for the illustrations and cover art. You nailed it.

ABOUT THE AUTHOR

As an unconventional rehabber with a meticulous focus on details and an abundance of wit, Mark Russell is devoted to elevating the goodness in every home he meets. It took a childhood interest in building, eight years of engineering and architectural studies, and a 30-year career in department store merchandising to finally lead him to his life's calling.

As a storyteller at heart, Mark shares his adventures along with helpful tips in his book, *Past Forward: The Art & Science of Saving Houses*, a must-read for anyone who is thinking about getting into the rehab business or buying a rescued house.